BTEC Level 2 First Study Skills Guide in Art and Design

Welcome to your **···dy Skills Guide! You can make it**
your own – start **vour personal and course**
details below...

Learner's name:

BTEC course title:

Date started:

Mandatory units:

Optional units:

Centre name:

Centre address:

Tutor's name:

Published by Pearson Education Limited, a company incorporated in England and Wales, having its registered office at Edinburgh Gate, Harlow, Essex, CM20 2JE. Registered company number: 872828

Edexcel is a registered trademark of Edexcel Limited

First published 2010

13 12 11 10
10 9 8 7 6 5 4 3 2

British Library Cataloguing in Publication Data
A catalogue record for this book is available from the British Library

ISBN 978 1 84690 580 3

Typeset and edited by DSM Partnership
Cover design by Pearson Education Limited
Cover photo/illustration © Alamy Images: Asia Images Group Pte Ltd
Printed in the UK by Ashford Colour Press Ltd, Gosport, Hampshrie

Acknowledgements
The author and publisher would like to thank the following individuals and organisations for permission to reproduce photographs:
Alamy Images: Ace Stock Limited 56; Alan Parsons: 75, 76, 76/2, 77; Corbis: 61, Comstock 5; Victoria Dow: 13, 64; iStockphoto: 37; Pearson Education Ltd: Steve Shott 22, Ian Wedgewood 35; Kelly Thackray: 42; TopFoto: John Powell 18.

All other images © Pearson Education.

Every effort has been made to contact copyright holders of material reproduced in this book. Any omissions will be rectified in subsequent printings if notice is given to the publishers.

Websites
Go to www.pearsonhotlinks.co.uk to gain access to the relevant website links and information on how they can aid your studies. When you access the site, search for either the express code 5803S, title BTEC Level 2 First Study Skills Guide in Art and Design or ISBN 9781846905803.

Disclaimer
This material has been published on behalf of Edexcel and offers high-quality support for the delivery of Edexcel qualifications.
This does not mean that the material is essential to achieve any Edexcel qualification, nor does it mean that it is the only suitable material available to support any Edexcel qualification. Edexcel material will not be used verbatim in setting any Edexcel examination or assessment. Any resource lists produced by Edexcel shall include this and other appropriate resources. Copies of official specifications for all Edexcel qualifications may be found on the Edexcel website: www.edexcel.com

Contents

Popular progression pathways

General qualification	Vocationally related qualification	Applied qualification
Undergraduate Degree	BTEC Higher National	Foundation Degree
GCE AS and A level	BTEC National	Advanced Diploma
GCSE	BTEC First	Higher (L2) and Foundation (L1) Diplomas

Your BTEC First course
Early days

Every year many new learners start BTEC Level 2 First courses, enjoy the challenge and successfully achieve their award. Some do this the easy way; others make it harder for themselves.

Everyone will have different feelings when they start their course.

Case study: Using this guide

Liam is about to start a BTEC First in Art and Design and he begins to think about what it might mean to be a creative studies student.

His portfolio of work was good enough to get him a study place. He knows he is quite good at drawing and painting but, in looking round the design studios and talking with friends, Liam realises that there might be so much more to studying art and design. He wonders how he can discover more about what is in store on a BTEC First.

He talks to his tutor, who tells Liam to imagine himself as a traveller in a strange country. She asks him what would be the one thing he would always carry with him on his travels. Liam struggles to think of an answer so his tutor tells him what she is thinking of: "Your travel guide, of course – an essential source of information about where you are, what you will find when you begin to explore, how you can find out more about where your journey could lead to."

Liam's tutor goes on to explain that the *BTEC First Study Skills Guide* serves a similar purpose. It is a source of information about his course and clarifies how he could get the most from a BTEC Art and Design qualification.

She explains that the guide includes case studies that will help him to find out more about what it means to be an artist and a designer. The guide includes activities to help develop new skills and build confidence, and it offers guidance on how to study, research, plan and produce ideas and develop concepts. She concludes by telling him that the guide will offer direction on how to present his work so that others can judge his capabilities and assess his creative talent.

Liam will follow his tutor's advice and he intends to benefit from using the *BTEC First Study Skills Guide* during his BTEC First in Art and Design course.

About your course

What do you know already?

If someone asks you about your course, could you give a short, accurate description? If you can, you have a good understanding of what your course is about. This has several benefits.

Four benefits of understanding your course

1	You will be better prepared and organised.
2	You can make links between the course and the world around you.
3	You can check how your personal interests and hobbies relate to the course.
4	You will pay attention to information that relates to topics you are studying, whether it's from conversations with family and friends, watching television or at a part-time job.

TRY THIS

Write down your interests and hobbies and identify those that relate to your studies in any way.

Read any information you have been given by your centre. You can also check the Edexcel website for further details – go to www.edexcel.com.

Interest/hobby	How this relates to my studies

What else do you need to know?

Five facts you should find out about your course

1. The type of BTEC qualification you are studying.
2. How many credits your qualification is worth.
3. The number of **mandatory** units you will study and what they cover.
4. How many credits the mandatory units are worth.
5. The number of **optional** units you need to study in total and the options available in your centre.

Case study: What will I study?

Ali and Katy are really looking forward to starting their BTEC First in Art and Design. They decide to go to their tutor and ask for some information about the qualification.

Ali and Katy have impressed their tutor with their organised approach to trying to find out information. The tutor thinks that here are two students who will be well suited to the BTEC course as they have demonstrated a curious mind and a professional and confident approach to finding out information. The tutor tells the new students that their questions will form part of the first tutorial in their new subject. When they hear the word 'tutorial', Ali and Katy realise that their studies start with the introduction of a new style of receiving guidance.

The tutor also explains that information about the BTEC First in Art and Design could also be found in the student handbook, and she gives them both a copy. The tutor adds that their first tutorial would form part of the 'induction' aspect of their course, clarifying that learning about the qualification, its structure and the manner in which the course is taught forms part of their earliest study experience.

They are given a tutorial handout that explains that the qualification is made up of units, and these are divided into 'mandatory' and 'optional' units. The handout states that they will learn through practical creative activities, underpinned by tutorials, lectures and visits.

They discover that this practical work will involve a range of project-based activities, using several media and working across two and three dimensions. As well as drawing, painting and photography, they will be working with print, ceramics, card, wood, metal and plastic. The handout clarifies that they would also be set assignments, which would be assessed by specialist tutors. They understand that they will get feedback during projects and assignments, which will help them to improve their work and attain good grades at the end of the unit.

Ali and Katy agreed that it would interesting to be graded with pass, merit and distinction criteria rather than be awarded 'marks out of 10' or a percentage mark.

Activity: How well do you know your course?

Complete this activity to check that you know the main facts. Compare your answers with a friend. You should have similar answers except where you make personal choices, such as about optional units. Your tutor can help you complete number 9.

1 The correct title of the BTEC award I am studying is:

2 The length of time it will take me to complete my award is:

3 The number of mandatory units I have to study is:

4 The titles of my mandatory units, and their credit values, are:

5 The main topics I will learn in each mandatory unit include:

Mandatory unit	Main topics

6 The number of credits I need to achieve by studying optional units is:

7 The titles of my optional units, and their credit values, are:

8 The main topics I will learn in each optional unit include:

Optional unit	Main topics

9 Other important aspects of my course are:

10 After I have achieved my BTEC First, my options include:

Introduction to the art and design sector

Art and design are two words that, together, describe work which is creatively visual (art) and which has been created for a specific purpose (design).

Visual arts and design include:

- drawing, painting, graphics, photography, printmaking and video – sometimes described as two-dimensional (2D) art
- sculpture, architecture, interior design, product engineering – described as three-dimensional (3D) art
- crafts such as ceramics, textiles and glass.

Art and design can also encompass computer games, animation, fashion and performance.

Case study: Art and design specialisms

As part of their induction, a group of BTEC First learners have been told that there are individual pathways of study in art and design. They decide to find out more about their creative selves and about their study area. Together they devise a series of topics relating to different art and design specialisms which they plan to research. They anticipate that some of the answers will come from their research and some from their own preconceptions about art and design.

As a starting point, they decide to gather some information from various sources, including:

- libraries and learning resource centres
- galleries and craft/design centres
- magazines and journals such as *Design* magazine and *Creative Review*.

In tandem with this research, they devise two questions for their tutor about their course and about specialist art and design study skills. They hope that these might give them some direction and hopefully not take too long for their tutor to answer. These questions and the tutor's answers are given below.

What will we learn on a BTEC First in Art and Design?

'When you study art and design you begin, from the outset, to learn new skills in a creative context. The BTEC First in Art and Design is divided into units which you will study in a range of different ways. You will learn about visual communication techniques, covering mark-making (2D design) and making (3D

design). In the unit on contextual references you will learn about the work of other artists and designers. In exploring art and design ideas, you will learn how to research and explore concepts that relate to a specific brief. You will also be able to study a unit (or units) of your choice. Some of the optional units focus on a specialist area, such as graphics, photography, fashion design, textiles, 3D design, interactive media (film, games design, animation etc), visual arts and 3D design crafts (jewellery, ceramics, furniture etc).'

How will we study on a BTEC First in Art and Design?

'You will learn in new and exciting ways, such as using contextual research (looking at the work of other artists and designers) for influence and inspiration. You will learn new studio and workshop skills, visit galleries and exhibitions, and perhaps travel to different cities and countries sketching and photographing subjects that interest and attract you and which may be of use in your current and future studies.'

The tutor goes on to explain that artists and designers, whether just starting their studies or experienced practitioners, will keep all their sketchbooks and their research. All the work that learners do could be useful later on the BTEC First, and then on their next course(s), which might be a diploma or a degree in art and design, and could become part of their archived information and portfolios as professional artists and designers.

Skills you need for your sector

Studying art and design requires several essential skills, which will be introduced as part of the BTEC First programme of study. Skills development is always ongoing for every artist and designer, and helps expand knowledge, increase confidence and extend ability.

Allow the development and practice of essential skills to be a part of your everyday activities, to inform and underpin every assignment, and to influence the way you see things around you. This will help you record your information, investigate, experiment, communicate and evaluate.

Some **generic** skills required in art and design relate to:

- investigate and record
- experiment and communicate
- analyse and evaluate
- reflect and inform.

Some **specialist** 2D visual language skills in art and design are:

- mark-making
- sketching
- conceptualising (drawing)
- rendering
- painting
- image-making (photography, film).

Some **specialist** 3D visual language skills in art and design are:

- cutting
- joining
- constructing
- forming
- modelling (maquettes and production).

Formal elements – the language used by artists, designers and craftspeople – include:

- line, tone and colour
- pattern and texture
- form, shape, scale and structure.

Activity: An apple a day

To help familiarise yourself with some generic skills and elements in art and design, try to complete these tasks, which involve 2D and 3D activities.

- Take an apple.
- Now take an A3 sheet of paper and grid it into six equal, numbered squares.
- Study the apple and record tone, texture and content, perhaps with charcoal, pencils or pastels, in boxes 1 and 2 (mark-making)
- Look carefully at the apple and sketch the shape and form from two different angles in boxes 3 and 4 (sketching).

- Experiment with colour and media to recreate the apple's skin or inside texture in boxes 5 and 6 (rendering).
- Take six photographic studies of an apple and mount onto an A3 sheet of card (image-making).
- Make a 3D prototype model of an apple, which you plan to produce. Experiment with card, *modroc*, plaster of Paris bandage or modelling clay (3D conceptualising-maquettes).
- Make an apple in an appropriate material, such as ceramic, wood, metal, paper or fabric (production).

Here is a scaled-down example of a completed A3 grid to give you some ideas for your photographic studies.

Mark-making using soft pencil or charcoal and cross-hatching with a hard or soft lead.

Sketching different views, exploring mixed media and different effects to symbolise shape and textures.

Rendering to conceptualise the product's shape and form, using different media effects.

Here are some ideas for photographing apples in stages of decay. The apples in the photographs were left for 24 hours in a warm place. You could get some interesting shots to drop into the remaining two squares on your A3 six-grid sheet if you put them on a windowsill for 24 days. Two mouldy versions would complete a good photo study.

More about BTEC Level 2 Firsts

What is different about a BTEC Level 2 First?

How you learn

Expect to be 'hands-on'. BTEC Level 2 Firsts are practical, and focus on the skills and knowledge needed in the workplace. You will learn new things and learn how to apply your knowledge.

BTEC First learners are expected to take responsibility for their own learning, and be keen and well organised. You should enjoy having more freedom, while knowing you can still ask for help or support if you need it.

How you are assessed

Many BTEC First courses are completed in one year, but if you are taking GCSEs as well, you may be doing it over two years or more. You will be assessed by completing **assignments** written by your tutors. These are based on **learning outcomes** set by Edexcel. Each assignment will have a deadline.

Case study: Understanding the BTEC First qualification

Nathan and Kian have been friends since they were in primary school and now they are both about to start a BTEC programme. Glancing at their new student handbook, they notice that it seems to read differently from their usual subject timetable and qualification guidance.

Together they decide to study the handbook more closely, and Nathan suggests that they should try to map out information about their qualification as this will help them to understand what is different about studying on a BTEC course.

They decide to use diagram templates on their computer, in tandem with the student handbook, to record information which seems important and which shows the differences between a BTEC qualification and others which they have studied to date.

This proves to be a useful exercise. Nathan and Kian decide to share their diagram with friends, printing out a copy for them to put into their logbooks.

They pick out three headers from their student handbook to start the cyclical diagram.

- Structure – how many units make up a BTEC First qualification.
- Assessment – how their practical and written work will be marked.
- Duration – how long their course will last.

Structure

Unit-based
First Diploma
6 mandatory units + optional units

First Extended Certificate
3 mandatory units + optional unit(s)

First Certificate
1 mandatory unit + optional unit(s)

Assessment

Assignment-based
Assignment is mapped against unit grading criteria for pass, merit and distinction

Regular assessor written feedback

Duration

Usually BTEC Firsts in Art and Design are delivered over 2 years but this can depend on the centre ie school or FE college

It could be 3 years on a school timetable

Getting the most from your BTEC

Getting the most from your BTEC involves several skills, such as using your time effectively and working well with other people. Knowing yourself is also important.

Knowing yourself

How would you describe yourself? Make some notes here.

If you described yourself to someone else, would you be able to sum up your temperament and personality, identify your strengths and weaknesses and list your skills? If not, is it because you've never thought about it or because you honestly don't have a clue?

Learning about yourself is often called self-analysis. You may have already done personality tests or careers profiles. If not, there are many available online. However, the information you gain from these profiles is useless unless you can apply it to what you are doing.

Your personality

Everyone is different. For example, some people:
- like to plan in advance; others prefer to be spontaneous
- love being part of a group; others prefer one or two close friends
- enjoy being the life and soul of the party; others prefer to sit quietly and tend to feel uncomfortable at large social gatherings
- are imaginative and creative; others prefer to deal only with facts
- think carefully about all their options before making a decision; others follow their 'gut instincts' and often let their heart rule their head.

Case study: Starting your BTEC First course

Having established the BTEC First in Art and Design as being a different way to study, it is useful to try to relate personality to new methods of learning. It can be quite difficult to describe your own personality, so Liam's tutor offers his tutor group the chance to engage in a simple question and answer (Q & A) activity. To begin, they choose a partner to work with and the tutor gives each pair a list of simple questions to ask each other. They are told to jot down the questions and make a note of the answers. Here are the questions, with Liam's answers.

Do you like to sketch and doodle? *Yes*

How often do you sketch and doodle?
All of the time

Do you like to take photographs? *Yes*

What do you photograph?
Anything and everything that takes my interest

Do you ever sort out your sketches, doodles and photographs into any order?
No, never thought about it

Do you ever look at other people's work?
I sometimes go to an art gallery

Do you ever look at your friends' work?
Only if they ask me to

What do you see as important in learning how to study art and design? *Looking and listening*

How will you show others what you have learned?
By letting them look at my work

How will you save your work?
In a folder

The tutor tells the class that she has given them these questions in order to help them understand the sort of characteristics and habits that they need to develop during their BTEC course. She gives them a printout with some 'tips for the top', which she asks them to save, telling them that if they follow the actions it could help them to become successful artists and designers. Here is a copy of the tutor's tips.

- Be confident enough to use visual language to communicate

- Be creatively purposeful

- Be creatively curious

- Be able to learn from others

- Be willing to work hard, listen hard and demonstrate creative ability

- Be able to document your own work to demonstrate skills

- Be able to archive and store work in an appropriate format (e-portfolio, traditional portfolio, logbook, sketchbook, DVD etc)

TRY THIS

Imagine one of your friends is describing your best features. What would they say?

Personalities in the workplace

There's a mix of personalities in most workplaces. Some people, such as many IT practitioners, prefer to work behind the scenes so that they can concentrate on tasks they enjoy doing. Others love high-profile jobs, where they may often be involved in high-pressure situations, such as paramedics and television presenters. Most people fall somewhere between these two extremes.

In any job there will be some aspects that are more appealing and interesting than others. If you have a part-time job you will already know this. The same thing applies to any course you take!

Your personality and your BTEC First course

Understanding your personality means you can identify which parts of your course you are likely to find easy and which more difficult. Working out the aspects you need to develop should be positive. You can also think about how your strengths and weaknesses may affect other people.

- Natural planners find it easier to schedule work for assignments.
- Extroverts like giving presentations and working with others but may overwhelm quieter team members.
- Introverts often prefer to work alone and may be excellent at researching information.

Activity: What is your personality type?

1a) Identify your own personality type, either by referring to a personality test you have done recently or by going online and doing a reliable test. Go to www.pearsonhotlinks.co.uk, insert the express code 5803S and click on the link for this activity.

Print a summary of the completed test or write a brief description of the results for future reference.

b) Use this information to identify the tasks and personal characteristics that you find easy or difficult.

	Easy	Difficult		Easy	Difficult
Being punctual			Researching facts carefully and accurately		
Planning how to do a job					
Working neatly and accurately			Solving problems		
Being well organised			Meeting deadlines		
Having good ideas			Finding and correcting own errors		
Taking on new challenges			Clearing up after yourself		
Being observant			Helping other people		
Working with details			Working as a member of a team		
Being patient			Being sensitive to the needs of others		
Coping with criticism					
Dealing with customers			Respecting other people's opinions		
Making decisions			Being tactful and discreet		
Keeping calm under stress			Being even-tempered		
Using your own initiative					

2 Which thing from your 'difficult' list do you think you should work on improving first? Start by identifying the benefits you will gain. Then decide how to achieve your goal.

Your knowledge and skills

You already have a great deal of knowledge, as well as practical and personal skills gained at school, at home and at work (if you have a part-time job). Now you need to assess these to identify your strengths and weaknesses.

To do this accurately, try to identify evidence for your knowledge and skills. Obvious examples are:

- previous qualifications
- school reports
- occasions when you have demonstrated particular skills, such as communicating with customers or colleagues in a part-time job.

TOP TIPS

The more you understand your own personality, the easier it is to build on your strengths and compensate for your weaknesses.

Part-time jobs give you knowledge and skills in a real work setting.

Activity: Check your skills

1 Score yourself from 1 to 5 for each of the skills in the table below.

1 = I'm very good at this skill.

2 = I'm good but could improve this skill.

3 = This skill is only average and I know that I need to improve it.

4 = I'm weak at this skill and must work hard to improve it.

5 = I've never had the chance to develop this skill.

Enter the score in the column headed 'Score A' and add today's date.

2 Look back at the units and topics you will be studying for your course – you entered them into the chart on page 9. Use this to identify any additional skills that you know are important for your course and add them to the table. Then score yourself for these skills, too.

3 Identify the main skills you will need in order to be successful in your chosen career, and highlight them in the table.

Go back and score yourself against each skill after three, six and nine months. That way you can monitor your progress and check where you need to take action to develop the most important skills you will need.

English and communication skills	Score A	Score B (after three months)	Score C (after six months)	Score D (after nine months)
Test dates:				
Reading and understanding different types of texts and information				
Speaking to other people face to face				
Speaking clearly on the telephone				
Listening carefully				
Writing clearly and concisely				
Presenting information in a logical order				
Summarising information				
Using correct punctuation and spelling				
Joining in a group discussion				
Expressing your own ideas and opinions appropriately				
Persuading other people to do something				
Making an oral presentation and presenting ideas clearly				

ICT skills	Score A	Score B (after three months)	Score C (after six months)	Score D (after nine months)
Test dates:				
Using ICT equipment correctly and safely				
Using a range of software				
Accurate keyboarding				
Proofreading				
Using the internet to find and select appropriate information				
Using ICT equipment to communicate and exchange information				
Producing professional documents which include tables and graphics				
Creating and interpreting spreadsheets				
Using PowerPoint				

Maths and numeracy skills	Score A	Score B (after three months)	Score C (after six months)	Score D (after nine months)
Test dates:				
Carrying out calculations (eg money, time, measurements etc) in a work-related situation				
Estimating amounts				
Understanding and interpreting data in tables, graphs, diagrams and charts				
Comparing prices and identifying best value for money				
Solving routine and non-routine work-related numerical problems				

Case study: Personality self–assessment

In order to help all the learners in Ali, Katy, Liam, Nathan and Kian's group, their tutor gives them a list of statements that have been made by other students on art and design courses. The list should help the group get started with the personality self-assessment process. The tutor asks each learner in the group to try to relate the statements to what they know about themselves. They should also try to come up with their own ideas in response to the questions about art and design given in brackets after each statement.

- **Student:** I really relate to being able to express my ideas visually.
  (What makes me want to study art and design?)

- **Student:** I really like the idea of designing things which people will use or remember.
  (What made me choose art and design as a specific subject?)

- **Student:** I could learn to design products like mobile phones, hairdryers or furniture, cars, trains or even boats and caravans. I might design environmentally friendly buildings or eco-interiors, stage sets or television props, and develop special effects for theatre, film and television. Maybe I will design logos and graphic images, which will make people remember news and special events. Or

perhaps I could illustrate books or advertise sporting products.
(Why do I want to study a subject which involves learning new skills and tackling creative problems?)

- **Student:** I know that it is important to study the work of others in order to learn, and to assist with building my understanding of new materials and of how other artists have experimented with different techniques and ways of working.
  (Do I think I can learn from other people's work?)

- **Student:** Like any study option, success is really down to the individual: how hard I work, how well I listen, how I can demonstrate my ability and how I develop my art and design portfolio.
  (Can I be a successful artist or designer through study?)

- **Student:** My portfolio is the way in which I can tell others how talented and valuable I am. It is a passport to further specialist study and, eventually, successful employment. Like most things in life, you will only get out what you put in – if I include my best and most creative work, then I hope that everyone will want to know about me!
  (Will my work be recognised?)

Managing your time

Some people are brilliant at managing their time. They do everything they need to and have time left over for activities they enjoy. Other people complain that they don't know where the time goes.

Which are you? If you need help to manage your time – and most people do – you will find help here.

Why time management is important

- It means you stay in control, get less stressed and don't skip important tasks.
- Some weeks will be peaceful, others will be hectic.
- The amount of homework and assignments you have to do will vary.
- As deadlines approach, time always seems to go faster.
- Some work will need to be done quickly, maybe for the next lesson; other tasks may need to be done over several days or weeks. This needs careful planning.
- You may have several assignments or tasks to complete in a short space of time.
- You want to have a social life.

Avoiding time–wasting

We can all plan to do work, and then find our plans go wrong. There may be several reasons for this. How many of the following do *you* do?

Top time-wasting activities
1   Allowing (or encouraging) people to interrupt you.
2   Not having the information, handouts or textbook you need because you've lost them or lent them to someone else.
3   Chatting to people, making calls or sending text messages when you should be working.
4   Getting distracted because you simply must keep checking out MySpace, Facebook or emails.
5   Putting off jobs until they are a total nightmare, then panicking.
6   Daydreaming.
7   Making a mess of something so you have to start all over again.

Planning and getting organised

The first step in managing your time is to plan ahead and be well organised. Some people are naturally good at this. They think ahead, write down their commitments in a diary or planner, and store their notes and handouts neatly and carefully so they can find them quickly.

How good are your working habits?

Talking to friends can take up a lot of time.

Improving your planning and organisational skills

1. Use a diary or planner to schedule working times into your weekdays and weekends.

2. Have a place for everything and everything in its place.

3. Be strict with yourself when you start work. If you aren't really in the mood, set a shorter time limit and give yourself a reward when the time is up.

4. Keep a diary in which you write down exactly what work you have to do.

5. Divide up long or complex tasks into manageable chunks and put each 'chunk' in your diary with a deadline of its own.

6. Write a 'to do' list if you have several different tasks. Tick them off as you go.

7. Always allow more time than you think you need for a task.

TRY THIS →

Analyse your average day.

How many hours do you spend sleeping, eating, travelling, attending school or college, working and taking part in leisure activities?

How much time is left for homework and assignments?

Case study: Getting yourself organised

Peter and his friends had been given a brief for a short two-day assignment, which their tutor has written for the specialist graphics unit. Peter's friends choose to work in small groups to discuss the assignment, but Peter decides that he is going to work on his own. He goes to the library and looks in a few books and magazines for some information about logos. He becomes engrossed in a book about games design and only makes a few notes related to his assignment.

He goes home with the intention of finding out some more information about logos on the internet, but he logs on to Facebook first, surfs the website for ages and, without realising the time, falls asleep.

When he goes into the studio the next day, he sees that his friends have quite a lot of information in their sketchbooks for the logo design brief. Because Peter has not done any useful research, he does not have any useful ideas that he could develop. Just before he goes home, Peter has another read of the project brief and realises, with a shock, that he is supposed to hand in his finished proposals at 9 am the next day. He begins to panic, knowing that he has really wasted a lot of time since the brief was handed out and, through missing out on the informal group discussion, the deadline has escaped him.

Peter tries to jot down some rough ideas in his sketchbook and rushes through his presentation. He is unhappy with the small amount of work he submits. It is clear that his friends have used the two days well and that their presentations are much better than his own. His disappointment makes him realise that he should be careful not to waste time at the beginning of any project, no matter how long or short the deadline given on the brief.

TOP TIPS

If you become distracted by social networking sites or email when you're working, set yourself a time limit of 10 minutes or so to indulge yourself.

BTEC FACT

If you have serious problems that are interfering with your ability to work or to concentrate, talk to your tutor. There are many ways in which BTEC learners who have personal difficulties can be supported to help them continue with their studies.

Activity: Managing time

1   The correct term for something you do in preference to starting a particular task is a 'displacement activity'. In the workplace this includes things like often going to the water cooler to get a drink, and constantly checking emails and so on online. People who work from home may tidy up, watch television or even cook a meal to put off starting a job.

Write down *your* top three displacement activities.

2 Today is Wednesday. Sajid has several jobs to do tonight and has started well by making a 'to do' list. He's worried that he won't get through all the things on his list and, because he works on Thursday and Friday evenings, that the rest will have to wait until Saturday.

a) Look through Sajid's list and decide which jobs are top priority and *must* be done tonight and which can be left until Saturday if he runs out of time.

b) Sajid is finding that his job is starting to interfere with his ability to do his assignments. What solutions can you suggest to help him?

Jobs to do

- File handouts from today's classes
- Phone Tom (left early today) to tell him the time of our presentation tomorrow has been changed to 11 am
- Research information online for next Tuesday's lesson
- Complete table from rough notes in class today
- Rewrite section of leaflet to talk about at tutorial tomorrow
- Write out class's ideas for the charity of the year, ready for course representatives meeting tomorrow lunchtime
- Redo handout Tom and I are giving out at presentation
- Plan how best to schedule assignment received today – deadline 3 weeks
- Download booklet from website ready for next Monday's class

Getting the most from work experience

On some BTEC First courses, all learners have to do a **work placement**. On others, they are recommended but not essential, or are required only for some optional units. If you are doing one, you need to prepare for it so that you get the most out of it. The checklists in this section will help.

Before you go checklist

1   Find out about the organisation by researching online.

2   Check that you have all the information you'll need about the placement.

3   Check the route you will need to take and how long it will take you. Always allow longer on the first day.

4   Check with your tutor what clothes are suitable and make sure you look the part.

5   Check that you know any rules or guidelines you must follow.

6   Check that you know what to do if you have a serious problem during the placement, such as being too ill to go to work.

7   Talk to your tutor if you have any special personal concerns.

8   Read the unit(s) that relate to your placement carefully. Highlight points you need to remember or refer to regularly.

9   Read the assessment criteria that relate to the unit(s) and use these to make a list of the information and evidence you'll need to obtain.

10 Your tutor will give you an official logbook or diary – or just use a notebook. Make notes each evening while things are fresh in your mind, and keep them safely.

While you're on work placement

Ideally, on your first day you'll be told about the business and what you'll be expected to do. You may even be allocated to one particular member of staff who will be your 'mentor'. However, not all firms operate like this, and if everyone is very busy, your **induction** may be rushed. If so, stay positive and watch other people to see what they're doing. Then offer to help where you can.

> ### BTEC FACT
>
> If you need specific evidence from a work placement for a particular unit, your tutor may give you a logbook or work diary, and will tell you how you will be assessed in relation to the work that you will do.

> ### TRY THIS
>
>
> You're on work experience. The placement is interesting and related to the job you want to do. However, you've been watching people most of the time and want to get more involved. Identify three jobs you think you could offer to do.

While you're there

1. Arrive with a positive attitude, knowing that you are going to do your best and get the most out of your time there.

2. Although you may be nervous at first, don't let that stop you from smiling at people, saying 'hello' and telling them your name.

3. Arrive punctually – or even early – every day. If you're delayed for any reason, phone and explain. Then get there as soon as you can.

4. If you take your mobile phone, switch it off when you arrive.

5. If you have nothing to do, offer to help someone who is busy or ask if you can watch someone who is doing a job that interests you.

6. Always remember to thank people who give you information, show you something or agree that you can observe them.

7. If you're asked to do something and don't understand what to do, ask for it to be repeated. If it's complicated, write it down.

8. If a task is difficult, start it and then check back that you are doing it correctly before you go any further.

9. Obey all company rules, such as regulations and procedures relating to health and safety and using machinery, the use of IT equipment and access to confidential information.

10. Don't rush off as fast as you can at the end of the day. Check first with your mentor or supervisor whether you can leave.

Coping with problems

Problems are rare but can happen. The most common ones are being bored because you're not given any work to do or upset because you feel someone is treating you unfairly. Normally, the best first step is to talk to your mentor at work or your supervisor. However, if you're very worried or upset, you may prefer to get in touch with your tutor instead – do it promptly.

TOP TIPS

Observing people who are skilled at what they do helps you learn a lot, and may even be part of your **assignment brief.**

Case study – continued...

The butterfly project facilitator needed some presentation material to demonstrate the final stage of the three-stage design process. This involved presenting final design ideas for a butterfly, which could eventually be produced as an embroidered and embellished piece of textile art.

Now put yourself in the position of the students, and see if you can create a final design for a butterfly. Some ideas are given in the sketches on page 29. Start your work by using the large outline butterfly below these sketches as a template. Make a copy of this shape. You can enlarge it by scanning the image into a computer (your tutor should be able to help you to save it using the appropriate software).

Try to create an accurate concept, imitating the colours you intend to feature in the butterfly you are going to produce. If you are going to decorate the image with sequins, stars or beads, then gather some samples and stick these on to your sketchbook template. Your finished concept should be mounted on a sheet of card.

Make a list of the materials you need for production in the space provided below.

You might like to present your butterfly in 2D and 3D versions. Here are some initial ideas:

- present a 2D version of the design in colour
- present a 2D version of the finished design, adding any decorations to your 2D template

- make a finished butterfly in 3D (to an appropriate size and scale) – this could be trimmed, stitched, in full colour, and surface-mounted on card, fabric or a 'natural habitat' such as a leaf, flower or branch.

Case study – continued...

Use this opportunity to design at your creative best – be individual, wildly imaginative and, above all, experimental!

This can be described as a 'blue-sky' project activity – enjoy!

Working with other people

Everyone finds it easy to work with people they like and far harder with those they don't. On your course you'll often be expected to work as a team to do a task. This gives you practice in working with different people.

You will be expected to:

- contribute to the task
- listen to other people's views
- adapt to other people's ways of working
- take responsibility for your own contribution
- agree the best way to resolve any problems.

These are quite complex skills. It helps if you understand the benefits to be gained by working cooperatively with other people and know the best way to achieve this.

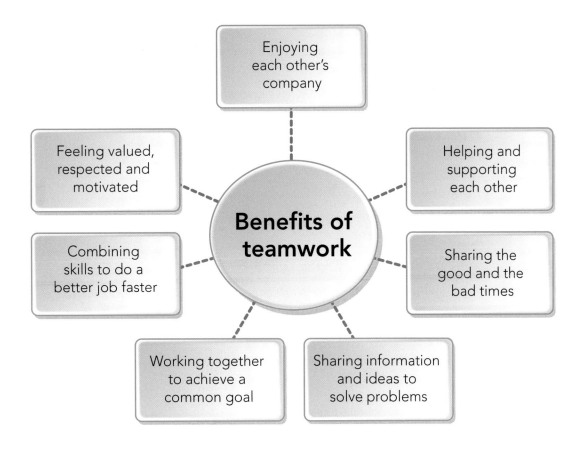

The benefits of good working relationships and teamwork

Golden rules for everyone (including the team leader!)

The secret of a successful team is that everyone works together. The role of the team leader is to make this as easy as possible by listening to people's views and coordinating everyone's efforts. A team leader is not there to give orders.

Positive teamwork checklist

- ✔ Be loyal to your team, including the team leader.
- ✔ Be reliable and dependable at all times.
- ✔ Be polite. Remember to say 'please' and 'thank you'.
- ✔ Think before you speak.
- ✔ Treat everyone the same.
- ✔ Make allowances for individual personalities. Give people 'space' if they need it, but be ready to offer support if they ask for it.
- ✔ Admit mistakes and apologise if you've done something wrong – learn from it but don't dwell on it.
- ✔ Give praise when it's due, give help when you can and thank people who help you.
- ✔ Keep confidences, and any promises that you make.

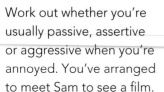

TRY THIS

Work out whether you're usually passive, assertive or aggressive when you're annoyed. You've arranged to meet Sam to see a film. He arrives 20 minutes late.

Do you:

a) shrug and say nothing in case he gets upset

b) ask why he didn't text you to give you warning

c) say that it's the last time you'll ever go anywhere with him and walk off?

Which do you think would be the most effective – and why?

Case study: Working with different people

Ali, Katy, Liam, Nathan and Kian are working on a group project. They have been set a similar task to the students who worked on the butterfly project. Their tutor has helped them by identifying some important points about working with others, and has asked the group to try to relate these points to art and design.

The tutor explains that each specialist creative study pathway involves working with different types of people. She suggests that the group should make a list of the type of people they might find themselves working with on a BTEC First in Art and Design. The tutor explains that the learners are likely to have contact with these groups throughout their studies and, indeed, their careers. This is the list the group produced.

In school or college
Art and media tutors
Specialist tutors and technicians
Friends and peers
External visitors

Work-related learning
Clients
Other artists and designers
Manufacturers
Engineers
Architects
Curators

Social-related
Friends
Peers
Other artists and designers

There are many benefits to be gained from working as a team.

Activity: Reflecting on working with others

Reflect on any work experience that you may have been involved in directly or consider the butterfly project case study to complete these tasks. This will help you appreciate what you may have learned about working with others.

If you have had a relevant work experience, describe what was it like to work with a real client. If not, what do you think it would have been like to work on the butterfly project?
20 words
What were/do you think would be the best experiences?
20 words
What were/could be the worst experiences and how/why did these happen?
20 words
How can you make sure the good points happen again?
List five ways
1
2
3
4
5

List five advantages in interacting with friends, peers, other artists and designers.

1

2

3

4

5

Getting the most from special events

BTEC First courses usually include several practical activities and special events. These enable you to find out information, develop your skills and knowledge in new situations and enjoy new experiences. They may include visits to external venues, visits from specialist speakers, and team events.

Visits to museums such as the Louvre in Paris may inspire you.

Most learners enjoy the chance to do something different. You'll probably look forward to some events more than others. If you're ready to get actively involved, you'll usually gain the most benefit. It also helps to make a few preparations!

Case study: Visiting a gallery

Nick is going to visit a gallery as part of his BTEC First. His tutor has told him that the experience should prove invaluable in learning about the work of other artists and designers. It will be particularly useful for Unit 1: Contextual References in Art and Design. His tutor suggests that Nick thinks about how his learning about the work of other artists could be referenced against his own thoughts and ideas (for essays and projects).

In order get the most out of his trip, Nick needs to plan and coordinate his time. His tutor gives him some basic pointers about getting the most from a gallery visit, telling him that he should list them in order of importance and add anything else which might help him benefit from his excursion.

His tutor also gives him a tip about recording information, suggesting that he use a small (A4/A5) sketchbook and try putting each pointer into a separate box or 'bubble' (this is called a bubble diagram). This could become his 'guide to visiting galleries', and he could also use the sketchbook

to record information (through written notes and sketches) during his visit.

Nick jots down this list of pointers:

- Getting there (travel details and map).
- Finding my way around the gallery (gallery map).
- Finding out who might advise and help on the day, such as gallery assistants, other visitors, and perhaps artists and craftspeople in residence at the gallery.
- Deciding on what and how much to try and see in relation to my course and/or project(s). I will need a gallery guide or exhibition catalogue.
- Recording information for future study through obtaining catalogues, making sketches and taking photographs (if the gallery gives permission!).
- Compiling a list of other related events, as well as people to meet and places to see.
- Writing letters, sending emails, making appointments in advance of the visit to be able to compile a schedule on the day.

Special events checklist

✔ Check you understand how the event relates to your course.

✔ If a visit or trip is not something you would normally find very interesting, try to keep an open mind. You might get a surprise!

✔ Find out what you're expected to do, and any rules or guidelines you must follow, including about your clothes or appearance.

✔ Always allow enough time to arrive five minutes early, and make sure you're never late.

✔ On an external visit, make notes on what you see and hear. This is essential if you have to write about it afterwards, use your information to answer questions in an assignment, or do something practical.

✔ If an external speaker is going to talk to your class, prepare a list of questions in advance. Nominate someone to thank the speaker afterwards. If you want to record the talk, it's polite to ask first.

✔ For a team event, you may be involved in planning and helping to allocate different team roles. You'll be expected to participate positively in any discussions, to talk for some (but not all) of the time, and perhaps to volunteer for some jobs yourself.

✔ Write up any notes you make as soon as you can – while you can still understand what you wrote!

 TRY THIS

At the last minute, you're asked to propose a vote of thanks to a visiting speaker on behalf of your class. What would you say?

Case study: Drawing a mind map

Nick knows that he can be quite disorganised, and he needs to improve in this area. His tutor has told him about mind mapping, and Nick decides that this process could be helpful in planning and coordinating his gallery visit. He remembers that the starting point that forms the centre (the core) of the 'map' is all-important, and that all the other related points branch out from this central 'core'.

He sketches out his gallery visit mind map in the inside page of the sketchbook that he is using to keep the rest of his pre-visit information and which he will use to take his notes and record visual observations while he is in the gallery itself.

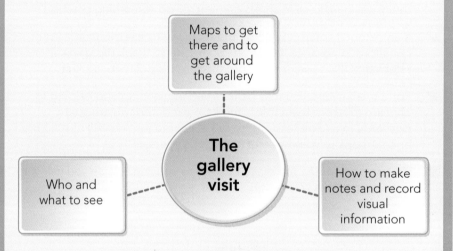

Nick's first attempt at mind mapping (see above) is very simple. So, imagine that you are going to visit a gallery like Tate Modern in London and try to develop Nick's basic mind map by adding more detail and adding in some more branches to illustrate how the visit could be organised. For example, your mind map might detail:

- how to get to the gallery
- how to find the best way round the gallery
- who and what to see
- how to make notes
- how to record visual information.

Do not worry too much about drawing a 'perfect' circle, just let your mind 'map'.

Resources and research

Understanding resources

Resources are items that help you do something. The most obvious one is money! To obtain your BTEC First award, however, your resources are rather different.

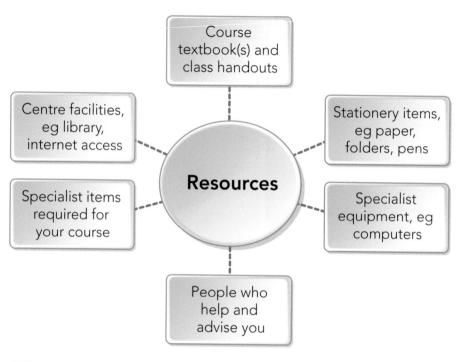

Different kinds of resources

Physical resources

Physical resources are things like textbooks, computers and any specialist equipment.

- Popular textbooks, laptops for home use and specialist equipment may need to be booked. Leaving it until the last minute is risky.
- You can ask for help if you don't know how to use resources properly.
- You should check what stationery and equipment you need at the start of your course and make sure you have it.
- You need to look after your resources carefully. This saves money and time spent replacing lost items.

People as resources

There are many people who can help you through your course:
- family members who help and support you
- your tutor

- friends in your group who collect handouts for you and phone you to keep you up to date when you're absent
- librarians and computer technicians at your centre or your local library
- expert practitioners.

Expert practitioners

Expert practitioners have worked hard to be successful in their chosen area. They know the skills and knowledge needed to do the job properly. They can be invaluable when you're researching information (see page 45). You can also learn a lot by watching them at work, especially if you can ask them questions about what they do, what they find hard and any difficulties they've had.

It is worth taking a closer look at how a practitioner works

Try to observe more than one expert practitioner:

- It gives you a better picture about what they do.
- No single job will cover all aspects of work that might apply to your studies.
- You may find some experts more approachable and easy to understand than others. For example, if someone is impatient because they're busy it may be difficult to ask them questions, or if someone works very quickly, you may find it hard to follow what they're doing.

If you have problems, just note what you've learned and compare it with your other observations. And there's always the chance that you're observing someone who's not very good at their job! You'll only know this for certain if you've seen what people should be doing.

Create your own resource list

You are likely to want to get help from many people and use many specialist resources during your course. At this stage, therefore, it could be helpful to create a list of useful resources for future reference.

You can start this list in your course notebook, but perhaps the best way to store the information is electronically (on a laptop or computer). This is because this list will need to be constantly updated if it is to serve as a valuable reference source for you on your BTEC First in Art and Design and beyond. You should be able to archive the list in sections, and add new resources through your continuing studies and into your career. If this is done well, you will have an extremely useful designer's resource and reference tool.

Here are some ways in which you can store information on resources:
- in a workbook (in sections)
- in a course file (with dividers)
- on a computer (in tables or spreadsheets).

Remember that a resource list is something you will add to again and again, so you need to decide on the method of storage and recall that suits you best.

A productive way of developing a resource list is to divide the contents into several sections from the outset. The graphic below suggests ways of dividing the resources you might need into five main sections. You will have your own ideas about how to divide your resource list, but these headers may help to provide a starting point. Think about the type of information that you might hold under each heading.

People	Places	Bibliographical	Web-based	Other

Research is often private as well as shared, so as an individual activity try to list some useful resources under each header in the table. Here are some suggestions for each section to start you off in developing your own listing:

People
- The programme leader on the BTEC First in Art and Design
- The design technician in my school/college
- The design team in the organisation in which I am doing work experience (or the team I am working with on a live project)

Places
- Galleries
- Exhibition venues
- Libraries

Bibliographical
You need to find an appropriate way of referencing useful books, journals and periodicals. There are some internet-based tools that can help you make a bibliography. Go to www.pearsonhotlinks.co.uk, insert the express code 5803S and click on the link for this page.

Web-based

There are many useful resources on the internet. To get you started, if you go to www.pearsonhotlinks.co.uk, insert the express code 5803S and click on the link for this page, you will find links to two resources that you might find helpful. The first concerns ways of managing tasks efficiently and the second is a resource list for web designers.

As well as thinking about the main headers, you might also consider how your resource list could be organised into subheaders to make storage and retrieval easier. Try to add some subsections under each main header. This activity will help you make a good start to establishing an art and design resource list. If you start off confidently, you will go from strength to strength in sourcing and archiving appropriate resources and information. In time your interests may change depending on your study pathways and eventual career moves, but it is never too soon to begin creating a resource list.

People	Places	Bibliographical	Web-based	Other
Names and specialisms	Names and locations	Reference to author, title, publisher etc	Links to specialist sectors	Could include techniques, processes and technology links
Teaching staff	Galleries	Forty A – Objects of Desire: Design and Society Since 1750 (Thames & Hudson May 1992) ISBN: 9780500274126	Graphics	Could include tools and equipment needed on your course
	Libraries		Photography	
			Fashion	

Finding the information you need

The information explosion

There are lots of different ways to find out information – books, newspapers, magazines, television, radio, CDs, DVDs, the internet. And you can exchange information with other people by texting, sending an email or phoning someone.

All this makes it much easier to obtain information. If you know what you're doing, you can probably find most of what you need sitting at a computer. But there are some dangers:

- Finding exactly what you want online takes skill. You need to know what you're doing.
- It's easy to get too much information and become overwhelmed.
- It's unlikely that everything you need will be available online.
- The information you read may be out of date.
- The information may be neither reliable nor true.

Define what you are trying to find. (The more precise you are, the more likely you are to find what you're looking for.)

Know where to look for it. (Remember: the internet is not the only source of information.)

Recognise when you have found appropriate information.

Know what to do with information once you've found it. (Make sure that you understand it, interpret it correctly and record the source where you found it.)

Know when to stop looking (especially if you have a deadline).

Finding and using information effectively

Before you start

There are four things that will help you look in the right place and target your search properly.

Ask yourself ...	Because ...	Example
Exactly what do I need to find out?	It will save you time and effort.	If you need information about accidents, you need to know what type of accident and over what time period.
Why do I need this information and who is going to read it?	This puts the task into context. You need to identify the best type of information to obtain and how to get it.	If you're making a poster or leaflet for children, you'll need simple information that can be presented in a graphical format. If, however, you're giving a workplace presentation on accidents, you'll need tables and graphs to illustrate your talk.
Where can I find it?	You need to consider whether your source is trustworthy and up to date. The internet is great, but you must check that the sites you use are reliable.	To find out about accidents in the workplace you could talk to the health and safety at work officer. To find examples of accidents in your local area you could look through back copies of your local newspaper in the local library or newspaper offices.
What is my deadline?	You know how long you have to find the information and use it.	

TRY THIS

Schedule your research time by calculating backwards from the deadline date. Split the time you have 50/50 between searching for information and using it. This stops you searching for too long and getting lots of interesting material, but then not having the time to use it properly!

Your three main sources of information are:

- libraries or learning resource centres
- the internet
- asking other people, for example through interviews and questionnaires.

Researching in libraries

You can use the learning resource centre in your school or college, or a local public library. Public libraries usually have a large reference section with many resources available for loan, including CD-ROMs, encyclopaedias, government statistics, magazines, journals and newspapers, and databases such as Infotrac, which contains articles from newspapers and magazines over the last five years.

The librarian will show you how to find the resources you need and how to look up a specific book (or author) to check if it is available or is out on loan.

Some books and resources can only be used in the library itself, while others can be taken out on short-term or long-term loan. You need to plan how to access and use the resources that are popular or restricted.

Using your library

✔ If your centre has an intranet you might be able to check which books and CD-ROMs are available without actually visiting the library.

✔ All libraries have photocopying facilities, so take enough change with you to copy articles that you can't remove. Write down the source of any article you photocopy, ie the name and the date of the publication.

✔ Learn how to keep a reference file (or bibliography) in which you store the details of all your sources and references. A bibliography must include CDs, DVDs and other information formats, not just books and magazines.

✔ If your search is complicated, go at a quiet time when the librarian can help you.

✔ Don't get carried away if you find several books that contain the information you need. Too many can be confusing.

✔ Use the index to find information quickly by searching for key words. Scan the index using several likely alternatives.

✔ Only use books that you find easy to understand. A book is only helpful if you can retell the information in your own words.

Researching online

A good search engine such as Google will help you find useful websites. They look for sites based on the information you enter in the search box. In some cases, such as Ask.co.uk, you may get the chance to refine your choice after entering your key words or question.

Finding information on a website

Wikipedia is a popular free online encyclopaedia. It has been criticised because entries may be inaccurate as members of the public can edit the site. However, Wikipedia is trying to prevent this by organising professional editing.

If you're not sure whether something you read is correct, or if there is anything strange about it, check it against information on another site. Make sure you ask your tutor's opinion, too.

With large websites, it can be difficult to find what you need. Always read the whole screen – there may be several menus in different parts of the screen. To help you search, many large websites have:
- their own search facility or a site map that lists site content with links to the different pages
- links to similar sites where you might find more information. Clicking a link should open a new window, so you'll still be connected to the original site.

TRY THIS

Search engines don't just find websites. On Google, the options at the top of your screen include 'images', 'news' and 'maps'. If you click on 'more' and then 'even more', you'll find other options, too. You'll usually find the most relevant information if you use the UK version of a search engine. Only search the whole web if you deliberately want to include European and American information. To see this in action, go to www.pearsonhotlinks.co.uk, insert the express code 5803S and click on the link for this page.

There may be useful information and links at the top, foot or either side of a web page.

There are several other useful sites you could visit when researching online.

- **Directory sites** show websites in specific categories so you can focus your search at the start.
- **Forums** are sites, or areas of a website, where people post comments on an issue. They can be useful if you want to find out opinions on a topic. You can usually read them without registering.
- **News sites** include the BBC website as well as the sites for all the daily newspapers. Check the website of your local newspaper, too.

Printing information

- Only print information that you're sure will be useful. It's easy to print too much and find yourself drowning in paper.
- Make quick notes on your print-outs so that you remember why you wanted them. It will jog your memory when you're sorting through them later.
- If there's a printer-friendly option, use it. It will give you a print-out without unnecessary graphics or adverts.
- Check the bottom line of your print-outs. It should show the URL for that page of the website, and the date. You need those if you have to list your sources or if you want to quote from the page.

Researching by asking other people

You're likely to do this for two reasons:
- you need help from someone who knows a lot about a topic
- you need to find out several people's opinions on something.

TRY THIS

To see how directory sites work go to www.pearsonhotlinks.co.uk, insert the express code 5803S and click on the link for this page.

TOP TIPS

Bookmark sites you use regularly by adding the URL to your browser. How to do this will depend on which browser you use, such as Internet Explorer or Firefox.

Information from an expert

Explain politely why you are carrying out the investigation. Ask questions slowly and clearly about what they do and how they do it. If they don't mind, you could take written notes so you remember what they tell you. Put the name and title of the person, and the date, at the top. This is especially important if you might be seeing more than one person, to avoid getting your notes muddled up.

Ask whether you may contact them again, in case there's anything you need to check. Write down their phone number or email address. Above all, remember to say 'thank you'!

The opinions of several people

The easiest way to do this is with a questionnaire. You can either give people the questionnaire to complete themselves, or interview them and complete it yourself. Professional interviewers often telephone people to ask questions, but at this stage it's not a good idea unless you know the people you're phoning and they're happy for you to do this.

Devising a questionnaire

1   Make sure it has a title and clear instructions.

2   Rather than ask for opinions, give people options, eg yes/no, maybe/always, never/sometimes. This will make it easier to analyse the results.

3   Or you can ask interviewees to give a score, say out of 5, making it clear what each number represents, eg 5 = excellent, 3 = very good.

4   Keep your questionnaire short so that your interviewees don't lose interest. Between 10 and 15 questions is probably about right, as long as that's enough to find out all you need.

5   Remember to add 'thank you' at the end.

6   Decide upon the representative sample of people you will approach. These are the people whose views are the most relevant to the topic you're investigating.

7   Decide how many responses you need to get a valid answer. This means that the answer is representative of the wider population. For example, if you want views on food in your canteen, it's pointless only asking five people. You might pick the only five people who detest (or love) the food it serves.

TOP TIPS

Design your questionnaire so that you get quantifiable answers. This means you can easily add them up to get your final result.

TRY THIS

Always test your draft questionnaire on several people, to highlight any confusing questions or instructions.

Case study: Designing a questionnaire

Amy is a BTEC First student who has already impressed her teacher with the confident manner in which she asks questions of anybody and everybody linked with her study programme.

Amy's teacher decides to appoint her as project leader on an assignment to design and deliver a questionnaire about favourite artists. The whole study group is to be involved in designing the questions. The intention is that each learner in the group will take the questionnaire to students and tutors on other art and design courses in the college (and to anyone else who wants to join in the questionnaire activity).

As project leader, Amy decides that the best way to approach the task of designing a questionnaire is to ask the study group to make some suggestions through open discussion, and she asks her friend Beth to make some notes on a flipchart as they go along.

As a group, they decide, on the advice of their teacher, to limit the survey to around six questions so that people answering the questionnaire will not get bored. This is quite short, but the topic is simple and the potential audience is broad, so the information should be sufficiently detailed and useful to include in their contextual studies research folder.

Here are the points which Beth noted down following the group discussion. These eventually helped the study group design the finished questionnaire, which is entitled: Who is your favourite artist and why?

Give interviewees the option to choose up to three artists and ask them to grade them from 1 to 3, with 1 being their favourite.

1 Ask them if they can name their favourite artist's specialism – such as painter, sculptor etc – and allow them to answer 'yes', 'no' or 'don't know'.

2 Ask them to name the specialism, if they answered 'yes' to question 1.

3 Ask them if their favourite artist is 'modern' or 'traditional', asking them to answer 'M' for modern and 'T' for traditional.

4 Ask them to state where they heard about their favourite artist.

5 Ask them to describe why they like each of their favourite artists in one simple word.

How to store information effectively

You can assemble a considerable volume of information and evidence on a BTEC course. You must carefully consider the appropriate ways of storing this information as you begin your studies in art and design.

Studying BTEC First in Art and Design involves gathering a lot of information. This can be broadly related to three categories of study:

- contextual
- theoretical
- visual.

Contextual and theoretical studies involve gathering information on the work of other artists and on working practices in your specialist area of study in art and design. Visual information relates to the execution of art and design – in other words, the work you will produce.

Contextual research can involve:
- researching into the work of other artists and designers
- researching into historical periods and trends in art and design.

Theoretical research can involve:
- researching into the physical processes (methods) used in art and design
- research to develop a basic understanding of specialist processes in art and design.

Visual research can involve:
- project-based evidence (both 2D and 3D work)
- activity-related information (such as recording field trips, gallery and exhibition visits, foreign visits etc).

Contextual and theoretical research can be stored:
- electronically on your computer or laptop (in folders, zip folders and files)
- through web links in 'your favourites' on the web browser you use
- on DVDs and CD-ROMs
- in course journals, diaries and logbooks
- in sketchbooks
- in technical files.

Visual research can be stored:
- electronically on your computer or laptop (in folders, zip folders and files)
- on DVDs and CD-ROMs
- in course journals
- in sketchbooks
- in (electronic or manual) portfolios.

TOP TIPS

Organise the storage of your research from the very beginning of your BTEC First. The practice will stay with you always and will benefit you throughout your studies.

Activity: Researching your favourite artist

You have been given the task of researching your favourite artist as the first stage of a visual art project. Working on your own, try to complete the table below. Then discuss your answers with a friend to see if your shared ideas will be helpful in carrying out research.

Keep your answers relatvely brief at this early stage of developing an understanding of the ways of finding out information.

Why am I doing this research?	
What will I do with the information?	
Who is going to use this information?	
What sort of information do I intend to collect and why?	
Where might I source the information I need?	
When do I need the information by?	

Managing your information

Organising and selecting your information

Organising your information

The first step is to organise your information so that it's easy to use.

- Make sure your written notes are neat and have a clear heading – it's often useful to date them, too.
- Note useful pages in any books or magazines you have borrowed.
- Highlight relevant parts of any handouts or leaflets.
- Work out the results of any questionnaires you've used.

Selecting your information

Re-read the **assignment brief** or instructions you were given to remind yourself of the exact wording of the question(s) and divide your information into three groups:

1 Information that is totally relevant.
2 Information that is not as good, but could come in useful.
3 Information that doesn't match the questions or assignment brief very much but that you kept because you couldn't find anything better!

Check there are no obvious gaps in your information against the questions or assignment brief. If there are, make a note of them so that you know exactly what you still have to find. Although it's ideal to have everything you need before you start work, don't delay if you're short of time.

Putting your information in order

Putting your information in a logical order means you can find what you want easily. It will save you time in the long run. This is doubly important if you have lots of information and will be doing the work over several sessions.

Case study: Putting information in order

Ali and Katy's tutor decides to help their study group to begin to understand how important it is to organise information for purposeful study. She introduces her group to the concepts of information storage, archiving and retrieval.

She asks for two volunteers, and Ali and Katy come forward. The tutor explains that one of them will record comments on a flipchart and be responsible for making the notes clear enough for the other person to make up some PowerPoint slides to summarise the session.

Katy decides to head up the flipchart pages with the different information types provided by the tutor. This helps the whole group to focus their ideas.

Here is a sample of the pages from the flipchart recording the group discussion. The theme of the discussion is 'organising your information for art and design studies'.

Visual	Written	Electronic
Fix drawn or mark-making information which might smudge	Store project-related information in logbooks	Compressed files (zip) useful for storing visual content
Protect drawn work in clean paper sleeves	Keep a contextual and theoretical studies file	Laptop, PC, USB stick, DVD
Archive digital images on USB memory stick or DVD	Keep a health and safety folder and a technical file	Blackboard, Moodle
		Blackberry, iPod
		Multimedia storage
Spoken	**Performed**	**Artefact**
Audio tapes	Audio-visual recording through tapes, video, film	Digital storage
Mobile devices	Mobile devices	Photographic archiving

Interpreting and presenting your information

The next stage is to use your information to prepare the document and/or oral presentation you have to give. There are four steps:

1 Understand what you're reading.

2 Interpret what you're reading.

3 Know the best form in which to produce the information, bearing in mind the purpose for which it is required.

4 Create the required document so that it's in a suitable layout with correct spelling and punctuation.

Understanding what you read

As a general rule, never use information that you don't understand. However, nobody understands complex or unfamiliar material the first time they read it, especially if they just scan through it quickly. Before you reject it, try this:

Read it once to get the main idea.	Read it again, slowly, to try to take in more detail.	Look up any words you don't know in a dictionary to find out what they mean.
Write your own version.	Summarise the main points in your own words.	Read it a third time and underline or highlight the main points. (If this is a book or magazine that you shouldn't write in, take a photocopy first and write on that.)

Special note: Show both the article and your own version to your tutor to check your understanding. This will help you identify any points you missed out and help you improve your skills of interpreting and summarising.

Understanding unfamiliar information

Interpreting what you read

Interpreting what you read is different from understanding it. This is because you can't always take it for granted that something you read means what it says. The writer may have had a very strong or biased opinion, or may have exaggerated for effect. Often you can still use the information.

BTEC FACT

In your assignments, it's better to separate opinions from facts. If you're quoting someone's views, make this clear.

Strong opinions and bias

People often have strong points of view about certain topics. This may be based on reliable facts, but not always! We can all jump to conclusions that may not be very logical, especially if we feel strongly about something.

Things aren't always what they seem to be. Are these boys fighting or are they having a good time?

Exaggeration

Many newspapers exaggerate facts to startle and attract their readers.

LOCAL FIRM DOUBLES STAFF IN TWO WEEKS!

This newspaper headline sounds very positive. You could easily think it means employment is growing and there are more jobs in your area. Then you read on, and find the firm had only four staff and now has eight!

Tables and graphs

You need to be able to interpret what the figures mean, especially when you look at differences between columns or rows. For example, your friend might have an impressive spreadsheet that lists his income and expenditure. In reality, it doesn't tell you much until you add the figures up and subtract one from the other. Only then can you say whether he is getting into debt. And even if he is, you need to see his budget over a few months, rather than just one which may be exceptional.

Choosing a format

You may have been given specific instructions about the format and layout of a document you have to produce, in which case life is easy as long as you follow them. If not, think carefully about the best way to set out your information so that it is clear.

Different formats	Example
text	when you write in paragraphs or prepare a report or summary
graphical	a diagram, graph or chart
pictorial	a drawing, photograph, cartoon or pictogram
tabular	numerical information in a table

The best method(s) will depend on the information you have, the source(s) of your material and the purpose of the document – a leaflet for schoolchildren needs graphics and pictures to make it lively, whereas a report to company shareholders would be mainly in text form with just one or two graphs.

Stating your sources

Whatever format you use, if you are including other people's views, comments or opinions, or copying a table or diagram from another publication, you must state the source by including the name of the author, publication, or the web address. This can be in the text or as part of a list at the end. Failure to do this (so you are really pretending other people's work is your own) is known as **plagiarism**. It is a serious offence with penalties to match.

Text format

Creating written documents gets easier with practice. These points should help.

TOP TIPS

Don't just rely on your spellchecker. It won't find a word spelled wrongly that makes another valid word (eg from/form), so you must proofread everything. And remember to check whether it is set to check American English or British English. There are some spelling differences.

Golden rules for written documents

1 Think about who will be reading it, then write in an appropriate language and style.

2 Ensure it is technically correct, ie no wrong spellings or bad punctuation.

3 Take time to make it look good, with clear headings, consistent spacing and plenty of white space.

4 Write in paragraphs, each with a different theme. Leave a line space between each one.

5 If you have a lot of separate points to mention, use bullets or numbered points. Numbered points show a certain order or quantity (step 1, step 2 etc). Use bullet points when there is no suggested order.

6 Only use words that you understand the meaning of, or it might look as if you don't know what you mean.

7 Structure your document so that it has a beginning, middle and end.

8 Prepare a draft and ask your tutor to confirm you are on the right track and are using your information in the best way.

Graphical format

Most people find graphics better than a long description for creating a quick picture in the viewer's mind. There are several types of graphical format, and you can easily produce any of these if you have good ICT skills.

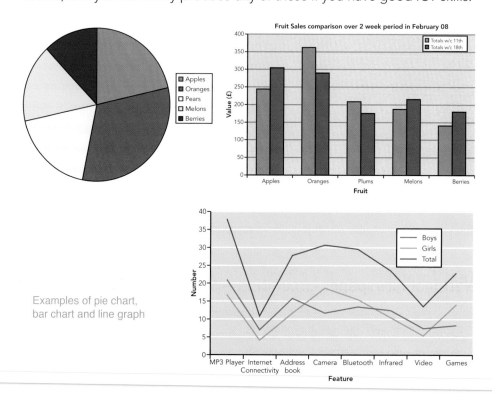

Examples of pie chart, bar chart and line graph

Pictorial format

Newspapers and magazines use pictures to illustrate situations and reduce the amount of words needed. It doesn't always have to be photographs though. For example, a new building may be sketched to show what it will look like.

A pictogram or pictograph is another type of pictorial format, such as charts which use the image of an object (fruit, coins, even pizzas) to represent data, such as the number eaten or amount spent.

Tabular format

A table can be an easy way to communicate information. Imagine a retailer preparing information about the items in stock. Text would be difficult to understand and comparisons between stock levels and sales would be almost impossible to make. A table, however, would easily show the fastest-selling items.

Tables are also ideal if you are showing rankings – such as best-selling music or books.

Bestsellers list – September 2009

Position	Title	Author	Imprint	Publication
1 (New)	Lost Symbol,The	Brown, Dan	Bantam Press	15-Sep-2009
2 (1)	Complaints, The	Rankin, Ian	Orion	03-Sep-2009
3 (New)	Return Journey, The	Binchy, Maeve	Orion	17-Sep-2009
4 (7)	Sapphire	Price, Katie	Century	30-Jul-2009
5 (9)	Wolf Hall	Mantel, Hilary	Fourth Estate	30-Apr-2009
6 (3)	Week in December, A	Faulks, Sebastian	Hutchinson	03-Sep-2009
7 (2	Alex Cross's Trial	Patterson, James	Century	10-Sep-2009
8 (4)	White Queen, The	Gregory, Philippa	Simon & Schuster Ltd	18-Aug-2009
9 (5)	Even Money	Francis, Dick & Francis, Felix	Michael Joseph	03-Sep-2009
10 (8)	206 Bones	Reichs, Kathy	William Heinemann	27-Aug-2009

National newspaper circulation – September 2009

	August 2009	August 2008	% change on last year	August 09 (without bulks)	March 2009 – August 2009	% change on last year
Sun	3,128,501	3,148,792	-0.64	3,128,501	3,052,480	-2.25
Daily Mail	2,171,686	2,258,843	-3.86	2,044,079	2,178,462	-4.45
Daily Mirror	1,324,883	1,455,270	-8.96	1,324,883	1,331,108	9.44
Daily Star	886,814	751,494	18.01	886,814	855,511	16.65
The Daily Telegraph	814,087	860,298	-5.37	722,644	807,328	-6.73
Daily Express	730,234	748,664	-2.46	730,234	727,824	-1.32
Times	576,185	612,779	-5.97	529,746	588,471	-4.63
Financial Times	395,845	417,570	-5.2	365,269	411,098	-6.7
Daily Record	347,302	390,197	-10.99	345,277	350,306	-10.59
Guardian	311,387	332,587	-6.37	311,387	332,790	-4.11
Independent	187,837	230,033	-18.34	148,551	198,445	-16.76

Activity: Mind mapping

Mind mapping is a diagrammatic method for organising information about almost anything. Nick used mind mapping as a method for planning his gallery trip (see page 40). In this activity, use mind mapping to produce a matrix to help you organise your course information. Here are some pointers.

1 See mind mapping as a shortcut to help you organise information for project planning, revision, evaluation etc.

2 Use mind mapping as an easy way to harness your imagination, and allow your brain to focus on organising your information.

3 Allow mind mapping to help you understand the focus and breadth of your information-gathering.

To mind-map, you need your imagination, some paper and coloured pens. You can use the outline map below or draw another. You can use any colour for any branch, but remember to label each branch. You can add pictures at the end of each branch. This may seem quite complicated, but remember that artists and designers need to organise many different types of information.

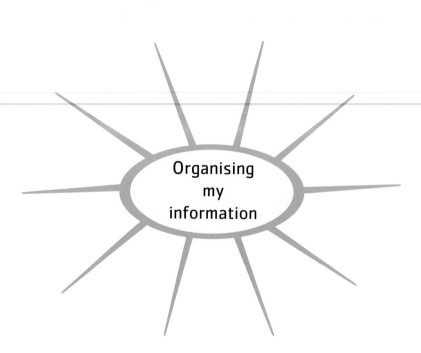

Organising my information

Making presentations

Presentations help you to learn communication skills.

Some people hate the idea of standing up to speak in front of an audience. This is quite normal, and you can use the extra energy from nerves to improve your performance.

Presentations aren't some form of torture devised by your tutor! They are included in your course because they help you learn many skills, such as speaking in public and preparing visual aids. They also help you practise working as a team member and give you a practical reason for researching information. And it can be far more enjoyable to talk about what you've found out rather than write about it!

There's a knack to preparing and giving a presentation so that you use your energies well, don't waste time, don't fall out with everyone around you and keep your stress levels as low as possible. Think about the task in three stages: preparation, organisation and delivery.

Preparation

Start your initial preparations as soon as you can. Putting them off will only cause problems later. Discuss the task in your team so that everyone is clear about what has to be done and how long you have to do it in.

Divide any research fairly among the team, allowing for people's strengths and weaknesses. You'll also need to agree:

- which visual aids would be best
- which handouts you need and who should prepare them
- where and when the presentation will be held, and what you should wear
- what questions you might be asked, both individually and as a team, and how you should prepare for them.

Once you've decided all this, carry out the tasks you've been allocated to the best of your ability and by the deadline agreed.

TOP TIPS

Keep visual aids simple but effective and check any handouts carefully before you make lots of copies.

Organisation

This is about the planning you need to do as a team so that everything will run smoothly on the day.

Delivery

This refers to your performance during the presentation. Being well prepared and well organised helps stop you panicking. If you're very nervous at the start, take a few deep breaths and concentrate on the task, not yourself. It's quite normal to be nervous at the start but this usually fades once you get under way. You might even enjoy it...

Presenting an art and design outcome

In art and design, you will spend a lot of time interpreting and presenting information, ideas and outcomes, in both visual and written formats. You will present to your peers, to your tutors, to people involved in work-based activities related to your course(s) and to parties involved in making decisions about your progression to further and higher education qualifications. As an artist and designer, you will work with a range of people who see and make decisions about your work.

As learners, you will be involved in activities and assignments where:
- you are presenting sketchbooks and development work for interim feedback
- you are presenting finished project outcomes for assessment and grading.

As a trainee artist and designer you will be involved in activities where:
- you are presenting sketch and concept development work for feedback from the rest of the design team or from a client to help you progress ideas relating to a specific project
- you are presenting finished project outcomes for team/client approval
- you are presenting work for consideration by others, where for example your work is being considered for inclusion in an exhibition or for sale.

In the creative industries there is an expectation that artists and designers will present both written and visual information to their peers, tutors, colleagues and potential clients. To do this successfully:
- you will need to understand the information you are presenting and be able to interpret decisions which affect your outcomes
- you will need to choose appropriate methods and media for the presentation of your information
- you will need to present work in a written and visual format that can be interpreted and understood by yourself and others.

Activity: Presenting and interpreting information

Here is an activity to help you interpret and present your information. It is about identifying the key points for interpreting your own work and for the presentation of any visual art project.

List three different ways of presenting art and design work, such as 2D mounted flatwork

Describe three different materials and/or media you might use for presenting finished work, such as digital images (photographs)

Think of three ways to present your interpretation of ideas and concepts, such as a project diary

Activity: Commenting on other people's work

This activity is about studying some images of others' work and making a brief comment about:

◉ the way in which the work has been presented

◉ how you might have presented it.

What do I think about this presentation?

What might I have done differently to present this work?

Your assessments

The importance of assignments

All learners on BTEC First courses are assessed by means of **assignments**. Each one is designed to link to specific **learning outcomes** and **grading criteria**. At the end of the course, your assignment grades put together determine your overall grade.

To get the best grade you can, you need to know the golden rules that apply to all assignments, then how to interpret the specific instructions.

10 golden rules for assignments

1. Check that you understand the instructions.

2. Check whether you have to do all the work on your own, or if you will do some as a member of a group. If you work as a team, you need to identify which parts are your own contributions.

3. Always write down any verbal instructions you are given.

4. Check the final deadline and any penalties for not meeting it.

5. Make sure you know what to do if you have a serious personal problem, eg illness, and need an official extension.

6. Copying someone else's work (**plagiarism**) is a serious offence and is easy for experienced tutors to spot. It's never worth the risk.

7. Schedule enough time for finding out the information and doing initial planning.

8. Allow plenty of time between talking to your tutor about your plans, preparations and drafts, and the final deadline.

9. Don't panic if the assignment seems long or complicated. Break it down into small, manageable chunks.

10. If you suddenly get stuck, ask your tutor to talk things through with you.

Case study: Christmas card assignment

A group of learners on the BTEC First in Art and Design has been asked by the principal to design the college Christmas card. They have been working in teams of four, and they now have to present their finished ideas to the principal and the dean of the school of design.

Their tutor explains that these are important people – in effect, the clients for this live project – and she advises each team to think carefully about who they will elect to present their work.

She reminds the learners of the information they have been given about presenting work, and she advises the presenters:

- to try and feel confident and knowledgeable about their team's work so that they can relax
- to look at their audience and engage their interest from the start
- to use good presentational techniques to promote their proposals
- to plan their presentation to maximise impact and avoid boredom
- to use simple and relevant language in their presentations.

The tutor also reminds the group of the importance of the visual material in the presentation – in this case, their project portfolio. She notes that a strong portfolio provides an open door to opportunity, praise and progress, but a weak portfolio can rapidly close it.

This tutorial before the presentations really helps the individuals chosen to making the verbal presentations. The reference to the project portfolio results in each team member deciding to make a brief comment about aspects of their ideas for Christmas card design and how these have been developed, leaving the finished proposal to be presented by the team's overall presenter.

The principal and dean of school are tremendously impressed with each team's presentation. They remark on how knowledgeable the learners are about their ideas, techniques and processes. The art and design teaching staff are delighted and praise the whole group for a professional presentation of a project well done.

Activity: Building a portfolio

Here is a simple activity to help you gain some insight into building an art and design portfolio.

Begin by trying to answer the questions on your own, and then compare answers with a friend. This way you can exchange ideas and thoughts and learn from each other, as there is more than one possible answer to each question. You will begin to understand that an art and design portfolio is a very individual and personal way of presenting creative work.

Q Is there a right or a wrong way to prepare an art and design portfolio?

A Yes or No

Q Name three ways of presenting a creative portfolio.

A 1

   2

   3

Q Choose one type of art and design portfolio. Briefly describe the benefits of this type of proposal.

A

Q What do you think should be a starting point in building an art and design portfolio?

A

Q Will you include a range of work in your portfolio?

A Yes or No

Q If yes, why?

A

Q If no, why not?

A

Q What do you think is the most important advantage of a developing a good art and design portfolio?

A

Interpreting the instructions

Most assignments start with a **command word** – describe, explain, evaluate etc. These words relate to how complex the answer should be.

Command words

TRY THIS

Check the command word you are likely to see for each of your units in the **grading grid** in advance. This tells you the **grading criteria** for the unit so that you know the evidence you will have to present.

Learners often don't do their best because they read the command words but don't understand exactly what they have to do. These tables show you what is required for each grade when you see a particular command word.

Command words and obtaining a pass

Complete ...	Complete a form, diagram or drawing.
Demonstrate ...	Show that you can do a particular activity.
Describe ...	Give a clear, straightforward description that includes all the main points.
Identify ...	Give all the basic facts relating to a certain topic.
List ...	Write a list of the main items (not sentences).
Name ...	State the proper terms related to a drawing or diagram.
Outline ...	Give all the main points, but without going into too much detail.
State ...	Point out or list the main features.

Examples:
- **List** the main features on your mobile phone.
- **Describe** the best way to greet a customer.
- **Outline** the procedures you follow to keep your computer system secure.

Command words and obtaining a merit

Analyse ...	Identify the factors that apply, and state how these are linked and how each of them relates to the topic.
Comment on ...	Give your own opinions or views.
Compare ... **Contrast ...**	Identify the main factors relating to two or more items and point out the similarities and differences.
Competently use ...	Take full account of information and feedback you have obtained to review or improve an activity.
Demonstrate ...	Prove you can carry out a more complex activity.
Describe ...	Give a full description including details of all the relevant features.
Explain ...	Give logical reasons to support your views.
Justify ...	Give reasons for the points you are making so that the reader knows what you're thinking.
Suggest ...	Give your own ideas or thoughts.

Examples:
- **Explain** why mobile phones are so popular.
- **Describe** the needs of four different types of customers.
- **Suggest** the type of procedures your employer would need to introduce to keep the IT system secure.

Command words and obtaining a distinction

Analyse …	Identify several relevant factors, show how they are linked, and explain the importance of each.
Compare … **Contrast …**	Identify the main factors in two or more situations, then explain the similarities and differences, and in some cases say which is best and why.
Demonstrate …	Prove that you can carry out a complex activity, taking into account information you have obtained or received to adapt your original idea.
Describe …	Give a comprehensive description which tells a story to the reader and shows that you can apply your knowledge and information correctly.
Evaluate …	Bring together all your information and make a judgement on the importance or success of something.
Explain …	Provide full details and reasons to support the arguments you are making.
Justify …	Give full reasons or evidence to support your opinion.
Recommend …	Weigh up all the evidence to come to a conclusion, with reasons, about what would be best.

Examples:
- **Evaluate** the features and performance of your mobile phone.
- **Analyse** the role of customer service in contributing to an organisation's success.
- **Justify** the main features on the website of a large, successful organisation of your choice.

TOP TIPS

Think of assignments as an opportunity to demonstrate what you've learned and to get useful feedback on your work.

Case study: Completing assignments

Liam has just completed an assignment, meeting the two-week deadline. The brief required learners to produce ideas for three ceramic tiles, depicting images in the style of Picasso, the artist Liam's study group is currently researching.

Liam carefully checks his project brief and gathers his research together. He puts his sketchbook alongside his written research, which he has collected in a file. He checks the annotations in his sketchbook and decides to put a red circle next to information he has logged on technical processes. He does this to emphasise that there are some references to health and safety, which demonstrates that he adopted safe working practices in his experimentation.

Liam then checks the grading criteria in his student handbook and tries to measure his evidence against the relevant criteria for this assignment. He looks carefully at his research and the development of his ideas in the context of the grading descriptors.

The descriptors for the pass criteria are basically, appropriately and safely. Liam feels he could tick off the pass criteria, especially with his brainwave to identify references to safe working practices with the red circle. He knows his research is relevant and he has put in some references to Picasso as a bibliography at the back of his folder.

The merit descriptors are effectively, consistently, range, alternatives, safely and competently. Liam feels he has worked really hard, planning the tasks and organising his work to meet the deadline. He has analysed his research carefully to develop his ideas for the ceramic tiles. He has made some maquettes to experiment with colour, and he has logged the process to prove he is able to work safely. He thinks he has met the merit criteria.

The distinction descriptors are creatively, independently, imaginatively, fluently, safely and individually. Liam really hopes he might be able to reach the distinction criteria when he used his project work to influence the design for his finished tiles in the final stage of the assignment brief.

TOP TIPS

Remember the golden rule for any art and design student – if you do not meet the hand-in date, you have not even met the pass criteria. A professional artist or designer who misses a client's deadline might not be paid.

Activity: Project briefs

To prepare you for a new style of working on the BTEC First in Art and Design, here are some frequently asked questions (FAQs) about projects (assignment briefs) and the processes relating to assignment briefs. Read these FAQs before attempting that tasks that follow.

What is a project?	A project is an undertaking. Project outcomes are presented for consideration, examination, feedback, assessment, analysis, evaluation and action. These activities are undertaken within a specific timescale.
What is an art and design brief?	An art and design brief is a way of communicating specific art and design requirements. A brief should include a title and a scenario (background). It will include clear timescales which identify the start date and the deadline for completion of the specified activities. The author of the brief should be named.
What is the art and design process?	The art and design process involves three main stages: research, concept and production. These are executed in a series of steps to meet a specific goal. Stage 1 involves analysis of the design brief, and conducting appropriate research to underpin initial ideas. Stage 2 involves analysis of the research, problem-solving and, producing concepts to illustrate the development of initial ideas. Stage 3 involves presenting solutions. This may be extended to include evaluation, and any action to resolve a criticism and/or meet any post-presentation amendments.

Consider these definitions in the context of this scenario. Suppose you have been asked to design a poster advertising a music festival in your town. The festival is called *All that Jazz* and it is being coordinated by the events team at the arts centre.

You have four weeks to work on the brief and your project must be handed in by the last day of October.

The poster will be A3 size, printed full colour, and must include a simple logo, which you will design specifically for the event. It must include the event date, time, venue location and the ticket price.

Now complete the table on page 72.

Describe the title and log the timescales and deadline.	
Describe briefly what the project is about.	
In your own words, briefly describe the art and design processes which might be involved in this graphic design and illustration brief.	

Sample assignment

Note about assignments
All learners are different and will approach their assignment in different ways.
The sample assignment that follows shows how one learner answered a brief to achieve pass, merit and distinction level criteria. The learner work shows just one way in which grading criteria can be evidenced. There are no standard or set answers. If you produce the required evidence for each task then you will achieve the grading criteria covered by the assignment.

Front sheet

Make sure you complete the assignment front sheet details fully and correctly; the details let the assessor and the internal verifier know who the work belongs to.

Make sure you know about the centre policy on meeting deadlines.

Ask your teacher/tutor to check over your assignment work and ask for some outline feedback on your work before handing it in.

Check the assessment criteria for your assignment tasks against the evidence you plan to hand in. Written work (annotation) and spoken words (presentation) support visual work, and both can provide evidence for assessment.

Learner name		Assessor name	
Nicholas Martin		Matthew Green	
Date issued	**Completion date**		**Submitted on**
30 September 2010	4 November 2010		4 November 2010
Qualification		**Unit**	
BTEC Level 2 First Diploma in Art and Design		Unit 3: 3D Visual Communication	

Assignment title	3D communication – model-making

In this assessment you will have opportunities to provide evidence against the following criteria.
Indicate the page numbers where the evidence can be found.

Criteria reference	To achieve the criteria the evidence must show that the student is able to:	Task no.	Page numbers
P1	demonstrate use of 3D making techniques safely when working from primary and secondary sources	2	See sketchbook and models
P2	communicate design ideas using 3D visual communication techniques	1	See sketchbook and models
P3	use formal elements in 3D visual communication	2, 3	See sketchbook and models
M1	demonstrate consistent and effective use of 3D making techniques when working from primary and secondary sources	2	See sketchbook and models
M2	communicate ideas effectively and consistently, using 3D making skills	1	See sketchbook and models
M3	explain the use of formal elements in 3D visual communication	2, 3	See sketchbook and models
D1	demonstrate imaginative and independent use of 3D making techniques, when working from primary and secondary sources	2	See sketchbook and models
D2	communicate ideas imaginatively and independently using 3D making techniques	1	See sketchbook and models
D3	evaluate the use of formal elements in 3D visual communication	2, 3	See sketchbook and models

Learner declaration

I certify that the work submitted for this assignment is my own and research sources are fully acknowledged.

Learner signature: *Nicholas Martin*   Date: *4 November 2010*

This table identifies the grading criteria and assigned tasks, and shows where evidence needed for assessment can be found.

Signing the document shows that the work is authentic (belongs to you), does not breach copyright and is appropriate for assessment.

Assignment brief

The scenario will help you relate the assignment tasks to the real world of art and design.

'Formal elements' are the item's parts and what it is made of. You will need to use the correct language to describe these.

Test pieces help you develop your ideas and make decisions about materials, techniques and processes.

Unit title	Unit 3: 3D Visual Communication
Qualification	BTEC Level 2 First Diploma in Art and Design
Start date	30 September 2010
Deadline date	4 November 2010
Assessor	Matthew Green

Assignment title	3D communication – model-making

The purpose of this assignment is to:
- be able to communicate design ideas using 3D visual communication techniques
- be able to use formal elements in 3D visual communication – model-making

Scenario

Artists and designers use 3D visual communication in their work in many ways. These include developing ideas for products and artefacts in 3D formats, such as models and maquettes. This is an important part of the design process as it enables the practitioner to communicate their intentions in a suitable 3D format for viewing by clients or interested parties. Models can be used to submit ideas and designs for architectural developments, for interior designs and for products.

A designer has produced a set of designs for a manufacturer of tools and household products. Your brief is to develop a set of models that show what these new designs will look like in 3D. The designer has requested that a larger-scale model is made to demonstrate the effectiveness of the new design.

Task 1

Choose a household item or common tool to research. The object you choose must have a joint or moving part, such as a pair of scissors. You should be able to draw and photograph the item. You will be developing a 3D model based on the item. Your research should include evidence about its history and the material used in its construction, and you should also include annotated studies showing the various forms that the item is made from. You can do this by identifying rectangles, circles and spheres, and other regular and irregular shapes in the object. and drawing these forms contained within the item.

This provides evidence for P2, M2 and D2

Task 2

Produce a series of test pieces to explore the potential of different materials to make a model of your chosen item. The model you will produce (for Task 3) should be a functional piece – that is, if the original item turns in some way, your model should also do so. The model should be larger than the actual item. You will need to scale up the item to produce your model – as a guide, use either a scale of 1:4 or 1:5. You can negotiate other scales with your tutor if you wish. At the end of this task, you should explain the suitability of the different materials that you have investigated for the construction of your model, the proposed finishing of your model, and which formal elements you exploited in your work.

This provides evidence for P1, P3, M1, M3, D1 and D3

Task 3

As a final outcome for this assignment, produce a scaled-up model of your item. The model should incorporate the formal elements and shapes contained in the original item. It should be produced in the materials you have chosen following your explorations and evaluations of different materials in Task 2. The reasons for choosing these materials should be given in your sketchbook or work journal. You should also evaluate your use of formal elements in your 3D visual communication.

This provides evidence for P3, M3 and D3

Sources of information

Collins J – *Sculpture Today* (Phaidon Press Ltd, illustrated edition, 2007) ISBN 978-0714843148
Lefteri C – *Materials for Inspirational Design* (Roto Vision, 2006) ISBN 978-2940361502
Fiell C – *Design for The 21st Century* (Taschen GMBH, 2003) ISBN 978-3822827796
Byars M – *New Chairs – Innovations in Design, Technology And Materials* (Chronicle Books, 2006) ISBN 978-0811853644
Hudson J – *1000 New Designs and Where To Find Them: A 21st Century Source Book* (Laurence King Publishing, 2006) ISBN 978-1856694667
Albus V, Kraus R and Woodham J M – *Icons of Design: The 20th Century* (Prestel Verlag, 2004) ISBN 978-3791323060

Websites

Design Council www.designcouncil.org.uk
Tate Online www.tate.org.uk
Victoria and Albert Museum www.vam.ac.uk

You can use this list of resources to help develop your ideas for the assignment.

Sample learner work

Using annotated research to record historical detail, and including illustrations of a relevant item in use, provides some underpinning evidence for M3.

Showing how the selected item was made and investigating its other uses provides supporting evidence for P3 and M3.

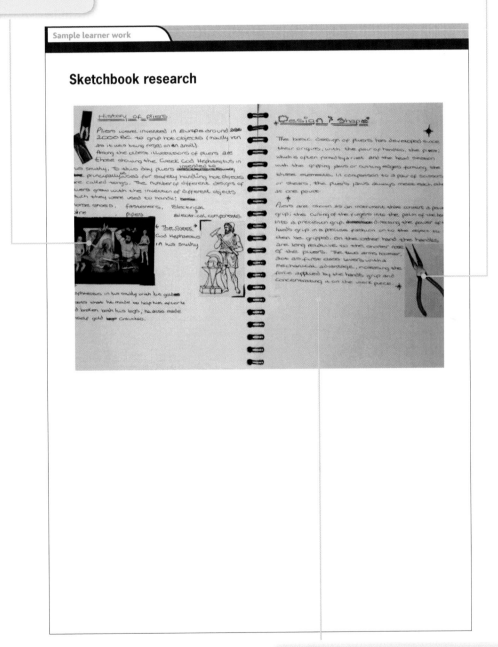

The learner has developed the range of primary and secondary evidence to support P1, M1 and D1. Primary resources relate to your own work and secondary resources are other people's materials from various sources, books, pictures, magazines and the internet, which the learner has stuck into the sketchbook.

This is a visual study. It records how your work develops. This sketchbook evidence will show your understanding of 3D form in your item and provide evidence for P1, P3, M1, M3 and D1.

The combination of sketchbook annotation on primary and secondary sources will provide evidence for the use of formal elements which will help the learner meet M3.

Item parts are well drawn and annotated. Information about modelling materials is included, and formal terms are clearly defined in sketchbook work. The evidence contained in the sketchbook supports P3 and M3.

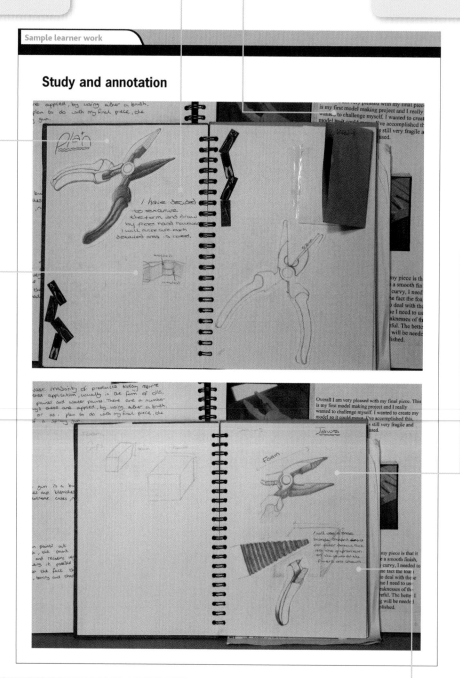

Sample learner work

Study and annotation

The detail in this thumbnail sketch will help the learner to explain the use of formal elements and will provide evidence for M3.

The learner has produced evidence to meet the criteria for use of formal elements (P3) and is able to explain the use of formal elements (M3).

The 3D model has been well made and presented with the original selected item which shows its scale. By demonstrating scale, the learner is showing that his 3D model is really accurate. D2 has been partly achieved here.

Sample learner work

Final model alongside original item

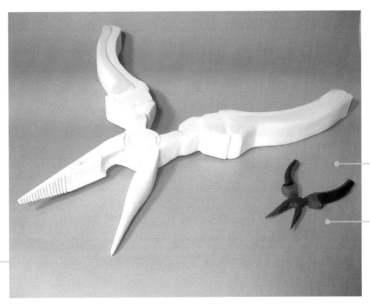

If the learner had worked on the visual and verbal parts of his presentation to demonstrate his thought process and ideas development more clearly and confidently, the M3 grading could have been improved to D3.

The standard of the finished 3D piece confirms that the learner understands scale and its application to a finished item of 3D modelmaking. The learner has illustrated an understanding of formal elements and scale in the finished piece by showing it alongside the chosen item (D2).

Observation record

Learner name	Nicholas Martin
Qualification	BTEC Level 2 First Diploma in Art and Design
Unit number and title	Unit 3: 3D Visual Communication

Description of activity undertaken (please be as specific as possible)

The learner was presenting his work at an end-of-assignment critique. He was asked to explain and evaluate his use of formal elements in the design and making of his final model.

Assessment and grading criteria

P1: use formal elements in 3D visual communication

M3: explain the use of formal elements in 3D visual communication

D3: evaluate the use of formal elements in 3D visual communication

How the activity meets the requirements of the assessment and grading criteria

Nicholas was able to explain his approach to using formal elements. He related his drawn work to identifying the component parts of the model. He understood scale and how he had applied it in the final model. His explanation was clear and used appropriate terminology. He acknowledged that his strengths lay in using the materials and developing craft skills. His explanation was sufficient to meet M3. He faltered a little regarding the evaluative aspect of his presentation. He did not develop his presentation to evaluate his choices of shape and structure in the final model. He understood that he could have applied different approaches in his making but did not produce any practical or verbal evidence to say that he had actually done this. His approach to the assignment was very practical. He understood that he could develop evaluation skills further – by thinking about analysing and evaluating in more detail. He also understood that to do this he would need to ask more questions about his choices of shape and structure.

Learner signature	Nicholas Martin	Date	4 November 2010
Assessor signature	Matthew Green	Date	4 November 2010
Assessor name	Matthew Green		

Assessor's comments

'Y' and 'N' mean 'Yes' or 'No'. This shows whether or not the evidence produced meets the grading criteria.

Qualification	BTEC Level 2 First Diploma in Art and Design	Year	2010–2011
Unit number and title	Unit 3: 3D Visual Communication	Learner name	Nicholas Martin

Grading criteria	Achieved?
P1 demonstrate use of 3D making techniques safely when working from primary and secondary sources	Y
P2 communicate design ideas using 3D visual communication techniques	Y
P3 use formal elements in 3D visual communication	Y
M1 demonstrate consistent and effective use of 3D making techniques when working from primary and secondary sources	Y
M2 communicate ideas effectively and consistently, using 3D making skills	Y
M3 explain the use of formal elements in 3D communication	Y
D1 demonstrate imaginative and independent use of 3D making techniques, when working from primary and secondary sources	Y
D2 communicate ideas imaginatively and independently using 3D making techniques	Y
D3 evaluate the use of formal elements in 3D visual communication	N

Learner feedback

Overall I enjoyed this assignment. I think the grading was fair and I agree with the tutor comments. I am going to resubmit my evaluation, analysing and reflecting on what I did in the model design and how I used formal elements. I have learnt a lot from the 3D workshop and about using foam.

Assessor feedback

(Grades achieved are shown in brackets)

Nicholas, you have worked consistently and safely on this assignment, following all relevant health and safety guidelines and legislation in the workshop (P1).

Your research skills were evident in your initial sketchbook analysis of the object, and you showed ability to communicate your ideas effectively, independently and with some imagination in your model-making. Your ideas about the mechanism and how to construct elements such as the jaws and pivot were imaginatively developed. You were able to work on scale drawings and develop a set of measurements for your drawings that you included in your key skills portfolio (P2, M2, D2).

You used a range of different 3D making techniques, including work in cutting and joining card in your early model making, and cutting, scoring, joining and fixing elements of your final foam model. Your interpretation of the working elements in the final model was well thought through and independently managed. You have a strong grasp of 3D making techniques, and you followed all health and safety guidelines independently (M1, D1).

You showed an ability to use formal elements in your model, and were able to explain the use of these in relation to the forms and 'component shapes' of your final model (P3, M3).

You could develop your analysis of your use of formal elements further, by evaluating them. You might consider questions such as:
• did you use the correct shapes to represent the forms?
• could you have improved the surface detail in any way?

And so on. You could also add the main things you feel that you have learnt about using scale to make a model. In this way you would be evaluating rather than just explaining.

You should always pay attention to the assessor feedback. It will help you to understand what has been achieved and what still needs to be achieved.

You should take the opportunity to give feedback on the assignment, for example what you enjoyed and what you found challenging. This is a good way of improving your work by thinking about how you did.

An action plan is a very useful tool in making progress. It shows you what you need to do in further work and keeps you focused.

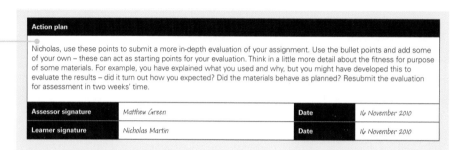

Action plan

Nicholas, use these points to submit a more in-depth evaluation of your assignment. Use the bullet points and add some of your own – these can act as starting points for your evaluation. Think in a little more detail about the fitness for purpose of some materials. For example, you have explained what you used and why, but you might have developed this to evaluate the results – did it turn out how you expected? Did the materials behave as planned? Resubmit the evaluation for assessment in two weeks' time.

Assessor signature	Matthew Green	Date	16 November 2010
Learner signature	Nicholas Martin	Date	16 November 2010

Coping with problems

Most learners sail through their BTEC First with no major problems. Unfortunately, not everyone is so lucky. Some may have personal difficulties or other issues that disrupt their work so they are late handing in their assignments. If this happens to you, it's vital to know what to do. This checklist should help.

Checklist for coping with problems

✔ Check that you know who to talk to.

✔ Don't sit on a problem and worry about it. Talk to someone promptly, in confidence. It's always easier to cope if you've shared it with someone.

✔ Most centres have professional counsellors you can talk to if you prefer. They won't repeat anything you say to them without your permission.

✔ If you've done something wrong or silly, people will respect you more if you are honest, admit where you went wrong and apologise promptly.

Case study: Student representation

Harmish and Rhian are discussing their BTEC First in Art and Design course and the issues they face with their studies. They realise that student representation might help learners cope with both study-related and personal problems. They decide to suggest the idea to their peers and tutors.

They put together a simple sheet outlining their idea, and call an informal meeting of their study group to consider the proposal. They politely send a copy to their programme leader to circulate to their tutors.

Although the meeting is informal, Harmish and Rhian decide that it would be useful to list some possible topics for discussion. This is their discussion list.

1 Do we need student representation?

2 What would be the ultimate value?

3 How would representation be organised?

4 Who would be listening to representatives?

5 How would we propose and elect individuals to act as representatives for learners on the BTEC First in Art and Design?

6 How often would our representatives meet with the rest of BTEC First study group?

7 How would they deliver their information and to whom?

8 How long would a representative's term of office last?

During the meeting the group decides that representation would be a good idea and it is proposed to elect two representatives by blind voting.

The group decides that one of the representatives should be a male student and one a female student as this would make it easier to deal with any personal problems. The group also decide to organise a monthly meeting, recognising that their elected peers would be a support to the full study group and could help to tackle any problems.

Activity: Questioning assessment feedback

Ashlee has a tutorial and receives feedback on her drawing assignment. Her tutor tells her that she is working towards a pass and, for some of the unit grading criteria, she may meet the merit descriptor.

Ashlee has worked really hard on her project and has included many examples of mark-making. She is really unhappy with her tutor's comments. After the tutorial, she looks through her assignment evidence and she still cannot understand why she has not already met all the pass criteria. She is unsure what she should do about her concerns.

Thinking about Ashlee's dilemma and reflecting on the information you have learnt about BTEC First courses so far, try and answer the three simple questions in the table below. See if you would be able to deal with a problem similar to Ashlee's.

Ashlee disagrees with her assessment; is there anything she can do about this?	Circle YES or NO in the box provided	YES
		NO
If yes, who should she approach first?	Highlight FRIEND or TUTOR in the box provided	FRIEND
		TUTOR
Do you think 'appeals' best describes the process of questioning assessment feedback?	Circle YES or NO in the box provided	YES
		NO

Skills building

To do your best in your assignments you need a number of skills, including:

- your **personal, learning and thinking skills**
- your **functional skills** of ICT, mathematics and English
- your proofreading and document-production skills.

Personal, learning and thinking skills (PLTS)

These are the skills, personal qualities and behaviour that you find in people who are effective and confident at work. These people enjoy carrying out a wide range of tasks, always try to do their best, and work well alone or with others. They enjoy a challenge and use new experiences to learn and develop.

Activity: How good are your PLTS?

1 Do this quiz to help you identify areas for improvement.

a) I get on well with other people.

Always   **Usually**   **Seldom**   **Never**

b) I ask for other people's suggestions for solving problems that puzzle me.

Always   **Usually**   **Seldom**   **Never**

c) I plan carefully to make sure I meet my deadlines.

Always   **Usually**   **Seldom**   **Never**

d) If someone is being difficult, I think carefully before making a response.

Always   **Usually**   **Seldom**   **Never**

e) I don't mind sharing my possessions or my time.

Always   **Usually**   **Seldom**   **Never**

f) I take account of other people's views and opinions.

Always   **Usually**   **Seldom**   **Never**

g) I enjoy thinking of new ways of doing things.

Always   **Usually**   **Seldom**   **Never**

h) I like creating new and different things.

Always   **Usually**   **Seldom**   **Never**

i) I enjoy planning and finding ways of solving problems.

Always   **Usually**   **Seldom**   **Never**

j) I enjoy getting feedback about my performance.

Always   Usually   Seldom   Never

k) I try to learn from constructive criticism so that I know what to improve.

Always   Usually   Seldom   Never

l) I enjoy new challenges.

Always   Usually   Seldom   Never

m) I am even-tempered.

Always   Usually   Seldom   Never

n) I am happy to make changes when necessary.

Always   Usually   Seldom   Never

o) I like helping other people.

Always   Usually   Seldom   Never

Score 3 points for each time you answered 'Always', 2 points for 'Usually', 1 point for 'Seldom' and 0 points for 'Never'. The higher your score, the higher your personal, learning and thinking skills.

2 How creative are you? Test yourself with this activity. Identify 50 different objects you could fit into a matchbox at the same time. As a start, three suitable items are a postage stamp, a grain of rice, a staple. Can you find 47 more?

Functional skills

Functional skills are the practical skills you need to function confidently, effectively and independently at work, when studying and in everyday life. They focus on the following areas:

- Information and Communications Technology (ICT)
- Maths
- English.

You may already be familiar with functional skills. Your BTEC First tutors will give you more information about how you will continue to develop these skills on your new course.

ICT skills

These will relate directly to how much 'hands-on' practice you have had on IT equipment. You may be an experienced IT user, and using word-processing, spreadsheet and presentation software may be second nature. Searching for information online may be something you do every day – in between downloading music, buying or selling on eBay and updating your Facebook profile.

BTEC FACTS

Your BTEC First qualification is at Level 2. Qualifications in functional skills start at Entry level and continue to Level 2. (You don't need to achieve functional skills to gain any BTEC qualification, and the evidence from a BTEC assignment can't be used towards the assessment of functional skills.)

Or you may prefer to avoid computer contact as much as possible. If so, there are two things you need to do.

1   Use every opportunity to improve your ICT skills so that you can start to live in the twenty-first century!

2   Make life easier by improving your basic proofreading and document preparation skills.

Proofreading and document preparation skills

Being able to produce well-displayed work quickly will make your life a lot easier. On any course there will be at least one unit that requires you to use good document preparation skills.

Tips to improve your document production skills

✔   If your keyboarding skills are poor, ask if there is a workshop you can join. Or your library or resource centre may have software you can use.

✔   Check that you know the format of documents you have to produce for assignments. It can help to have a 'model' version of each type in your folder for quick reference.

✔   Practise checking your work by reading word by word – and remember not to rely on spellcheckers (see page 57).

Activity: How good are your ICT skills?

1a)   Test your current ICT abilities by responding *honestly* to each of the following statements.

   i)   I can create a copy of my timetable using a word-processing or spreadsheet package.
   True   False

   ii)   I can devise and design a budget for myself for the next three months using a spreadsheet package.
   True   False

   iii)   I can email a friend who has just got broadband to say how to minimise the danger of computer viruses, what a podcast is, and also explain the restrictions on music downloads.
   True   False

   iv)   I can use presentation software to prepare a presentation containing four or five slides on a topic of my choice.
   True   False

   v)   I can research online to compare the performance and prices of laptop computers and prepare an information sheet using word-processing software.
   True   False

   vi)   I can prepare a poster, with graphics, for my mother's friend, who is starting her own business preparing children's party food, and attach it to an email to her for approval.
   True   False

TRY THIS

Learning to touch-type can save you hours of time. To check your keyboarding skills go to www. pearsonhotlinks.co.uk, insert the express code 5803S and click on the link for this page.

TOP TIPS

Print your work on good paper and keep it flat so that it looks good when you hand it in.

1b) Select any one of the above to which you answered false and learn how to do it.

2 Compare the two tables below. The first is an original document; the second is a typed copy. Are they identical? Highlight any differences you find and check them with the key on page 91.

Name	Date	Time	Room
Abbott	16 July	9.30 am	214
Grey	10 August	10.15 am	160
Johnston	12 August	2.20 pm	208
Waverley	18 July	3.15 pm	180
Jackson	30 September	11.15 am	209
Gregory	31 August	4.20 pm	320
Marshall	10 September	9.30 am	170
Bradley	16 September	2.20 pm	210

Name	Date	Time	Room
Abbott	26 July	9.30 am	214
Gray	10 August	10.15 am	160
Johnson	12 August	2.20 pm	208
Waverley	18 July	3.15 am	180
Jackson	31 September	11.15 am	209
Gregory	31 August	4.20 pm	320
Marshall	10 September	9.30 pm	170
Bradley	16 August	2.20 pm	201

Maths or numeracy skills

Four easy ways to improve your numeracy skills

1 Work out simple calculations in your head, like adding up the prices of items you are buying. Then check if you are correct when you pay for them.

2 Set yourself numeracy problems based on your everyday life. For example, if you are on a journey that takes 35 minutes and you leave home at 11.10am, what time will you arrive? If you are travelling at 40 miles an hour, how long will it take you to go 10 miles?

3 Treat yourself to a maths training program.

4 Check out online sites to improve your skills. Go to www. pearsonhotlinks.co.uk, insert the express code 5803S and click on the link for this page.

TOP TIPS

Quickly test answers. For example, if fuel costs 85p a litre and someone is buying 15 litres, estimate this at £1 x 15 (£15) and the answer should be just below this. So if your answer came out at £140, you'd immediately know you'd done something wrong.

Activity: How good are your maths skills?

Answer as many of the following questions as you can in 15 minutes. Check your answers with the key on page 91.

1 **a)** 12 + 28 = ?

      i) 30   ii) 34   iii) 38   iv) 40   v) 48

 b) 49 ÷ 7 = ?

      i) 6   ii) 7   iii) 8   iv) 9   v) 10

 c) ½ + 1¼ = ?

      i) ¾   ii) 1½   iii) 1¾   iv) 2¼   v) 3

 d) 4 × 12 = 8 × ?

      i) 5   ii) 6   iii) 7   iv) 8   v) 9

 e) 16.5 + 25.25 − ? = 13.25

      i) 28.5   ii) 31.25 iii) 34.5 iv) 41.65 v) 44

2 **a)** You buy four items at £1.99, two at 98p and three at £1.75. You hand over a £20 note. How much change will you get? _____

 b) What fraction of one litre is 250 ml? _____

 c) What percentage of £50 is £2.50? _____

 d) A designer travelling on business can claim 38.2p a mile in expenses. How much is she owed if she travels 625 miles? _____

 e) You are flying to New York in December. New York is five hours behind British time and the flight lasts eight hours. If you leave at 11.15 am, what time will you arrive? _____

 f) For your trip to the United States you need American dollars. You find that the exchange rate is $1.5 dollars.

    i) How many dollars will you receive if you exchange £500? _____

    ii) Last year your friend visited New York when the exchange rate was $1.8. She also exchanged £500. Did she receive more dollars than you or fewer – and by how much? _____

 g) A security guard and his dog patrol the perimeter fence of a warehouse each evening. The building is 480 metres long and 300 metres wide and the fence is 80 metres out from the building on all sides. If the guard and his dog patrol the fence three times a night, how far will they walk? _____

English skills

Your English skills affect your ability to understand what you read, prepare a written document, say what you mean and understand other people. Even if you're doing a practical subject, there will always be times when you need to leave someone a note, tell them about a phone call, read or listen to instructions – or write a letter for a job application!

Six easy ways to improve your English skills

1 Read more. It increases the number of words you know and helps to make you familiar with correct spellings.

2 Look up words you don't understand in a dictionary and check their meaning. Then try to use them yourself to increase your vocabulary.

3 Do crosswords. These help increase your vocabulary and practise your spelling at the same time.

4 You can use websites to help you get to grips with English vocabulary, grammar and punctuation. Go to www.pearsonhotlinks.co.uk, insert the express code 5803S and click on the link for this page.

5 Welcome opportunities to practise speaking in class, in discussion groups and during presentations – rather than avoiding them!

6 Test your ability to listen to someone else by seeing how much you can remember when they've finished speaking.

Activity: How good are your English skills?

1 In the table below are 'wrong' versions of words often spelled incorrectly. Write the correct spellings on the right. Check your list against the answers on page 91.

Incorrect spelling	Correct spelling
accomodation	
seperate	
definate	
payed	
desparate	
acceptible	
competant	
succesful	

2 Correct the error(s) in these sentences.

a) The plug on the computer is lose.

b) The car was stationery outside the house.

c) Their going on they're holidays tomorrow.

d) The principle of the college is John Smith.

e) We are all going accept Tom.

3 Punctuate these sentences correctly.

a) Toms train was late on Monday and Tuesday.

b) She is going to France Belgium Spain and Italy in the summer.

c) He comes from Leeds and says its great there.

4 Read the article on copyright.

Copyright

Anyone who uses a photocopier can break copyright law if they carry out unrestricted photocopying of certain documents. This is because The Copyright, Designs and Patents Act 1988 protects the creator of an original work against having it copied without permission.

Legally, every time anyone writes a book, composes a song, makes a film or creates any other type of artistic work, this work is treated as their property (or copyright). If anyone else wishes to make use of it, they must get permission to do so and, on occasions, pay a fee.

Licences can be obtained to allow educational establishments to photocopy limited numbers of some publications. In addition, copies of an original document can be made for certain specific purposes. These include research and private study. Under the Act, too, if an article is summarised and quoted by anyone, then the author and title of the original work must be acknowledged.

a) Test your ability to understand unfamiliar information by responding to the following statements with 'True' or 'False'.

i) Students and tutors in schools and colleges can copy anything they want.
True   False

ii) The law which covers copyright is The Copyright, Designs and Patents Act 1988.
True   False

iii) A student photocopying a document in the library must have a licence.
True   False

iv) Copyright only relates to books in the library.
True   False

v) If you quote a newspaper report in an assignment, you don't need to state the source.
True   False

vii) Anyone is allowed to photocopy a page of a book for research purposes.
True   False

b) Make a list of key points in the article, then write a brief summary in your own words.

5 Nikki has read a newspaper report that a horse racing in the Kentucky Derby had to be put down. The filly collapsed and the vet couldn't save her. Nikki says it's the third time in two years a racehorse has had to be put down in the US. As a horse lover she is convinced racing should be banned in Britain and the US. She argues that fox hunting was banned to protect foxes, and that racehorses are more important and more expensive than foxes. Darren disagrees. He says the law is not working, hardly anyone has been prosecuted, and fox hunting is going on just like before. Debbie says that animals aren't important whilst there is famine in the world.

a) Do you think the three arguments are logical? See if you can spot the flaws and check your ideas with the suggestions on page 91.

b) Sporting activities and support for sporting teams often provoke strong opinions. For a sport or team of your choice, identify two opposing views that might be held. Then decide how you would give a balanced view. Test your ideas with a friend or family member.

Answers

Skills building answers

ICT activities

2 Differences between the two tables are highlighted in bold.

Name	Date	Time	Room
Abbott	**16** July	9.30 am	214
Grey	10 August	10.15 am	160
Johnston	12 August	2.20 pm	208
Waverley	18 July	3.15 **pm**	180
Jackson	**30** September	11.15 am	209
Gregory	31 August	4.20 pm	320
Marshall	10 September	9.30 **am**	170
Bradley	16 **September**	2.20 pm	**210**

Maths/numeracy activities

1 **a)** iv, **b)** ii, **c)** iii, **d)** ii, **e)** i

2 **a)** £4.83, **b)** ¼, **c)** 5%, **d)** £238.75, **e)** 2.15 pm, **f) i)** $750 **ii)** $150 dollars more, **g)** 6.6 km.

English activities

1 Spellings: accommodation, separate, definite, paid, desperate, acceptable, competent, successful

2 Errors:
   a) The plug on the computer is <u>loose</u>.
   b) The car was <u>stationary</u> outside the house.
   c) <u>They're</u> going on <u>their</u> holidays tomorrow.
   d) The <u>principal</u> of the college is John Smith.
   e) We are all going <u>except</u> Tom.

3 Punctuation:
   a) Tom's train was late on Monday and Tuesday.
   b) She is going to France, Belgium, Spain and Italy in the summer.
   c) He comes from Leeds and says it's great there.

4 **a) i)** False, **ii)** True, **iii)** False, **iv)** False, **v)** False, **vi)** False, **vii)** True

5 A logical argument would be that if racehorses are frequently injured in a particular race, eg one with difficult jumps, then it should not be held. It is not logical to compare racehorses with foxes. The value of the animal is irrelevant if you are assessing cruelty. Darren's argument is entirely different and unrelated to Nikki's. Whether or not fox hunting legislation is effective has no bearing on the danger (or otherwise) to racehorses. Finally, famine is a separate issue altogether. You cannot logically 'rank' problems in the world to find a top one and ignore the others until this is solved.

Accessing website links

Links to various websites are referred to throughout this BTEC Level 2 First Study Skills Guide. In order to ensure that these links are up to date, that they work and that the sites aren't inadvertently linked to any material that could be considered offensive, we have made the links available on our website: www.pearsonhotlinks.co.uk. When you visit the site, please enter the express code 5803S to gain access to the website links and information on how they can be used to help you with your studies.

Useful terms

Apprenticeships
Schemes that enable you to work and earn money at the same time as you gain further qualifications (an NVQ award and a technical certificate) and improve your functional skills. Apprentices learn work-based skills relevant to their job role and their chosen industry. Go to www.pearsonhotlinks.co.uk, insert the express code 5803S and click on the link for this useful term entry to find out more.

Assessment methods
Methods, such as practical tasks and assignments, which are used to check that your work demonstrates the learning and understanding you need to obtain the qualification.

Assessor
The tutor who marks or assesses your work.

Assignment
A complete task or mini-**project** set to meet specific grading criteria.

Assignment brief
The information and instructions related to a particular assignment.

BTEC Level 3 Nationals
Qualifications you can take when you have successfully achieved a Level 2 qualification, such as BTEC First. They are offered in a variety of subjects.

Credit value
The number of credits attached to your BTEC course. The credit value increases relative to the length of time you need to complete the course, from 15 credits for a BTEC Certificate, to 30 credits for a BTEC Extended Certificate and 60 credits for a BTEC Diploma.

Command word
The word in an assignment that tells you what you have to do to produce the type of answer that is required, eg 'list', 'describe', 'analyse'.

Educational Maintenance Award (EMA)
This is a means-tested award which provides eligible learners under 19 who are studying a full-time course at a centre with a cash sum of money every week. Go to www.pearsonhotlinks.co.uk, insert the express code 5803S and click on the link for this useful term entry to find out more.

Functional skills
The practical skills that enable all learners to use and apply English, Maths and ICT both at work and in their everyday lives. They aren't compulsory to achieve on the course, but are of great use to you.

Grade
The rating of pass, merit or distinction that is given to an assignment you have completed, which identifies the standard you have achieved.

Grading criteria
The standard you have to demonstrate to obtain a particular grade in the unit. In other words, what you have to prove you can do.

Grading grid
The table in each unit of your BTEC qualification specification that sets out the grading criteria.

Indicative reading
Recommended books, magazines, journals and websites whose content is both suitable and relevant to the unit.

Induction
A short programme of events at the start of a course or work placement designed to give you essential information and introduce you to other people so that you can settle in easily.

Internal verification
The quality checks carried out by nominated tutors at all centres to ensure that all assignments are at the right level and cover appropriate learning outcomes. The checks also ensure that all **assessors** are marking work consistently and to the same standards.

Learning outcomes

The learning and skills you must demonstrate to show that you have learned a unit effectively.

Levels of study

The depth, breadth and complexity of knowledge, understanding and skills required to achieve a qualification determines its level. Level 2 is equivalent to GCSE level (grades A* to C). Level 3 equates to GCE A-level. As you successfully achieve one level, you can progress on to the next. BTEC qualifications are offered at Entry Level, then Levels 1, 2, 3, 4, 5, 6 and 7.

Mandatory units

On a BTEC Level 2 First course, these are the compulsory units that all learners must complete to gain the qualification.

Optional units

Units on your course from which you may be able to make a choice. They help you specialise your skills, knowledge and understanding, and may help progression into work or further education.

Personal, learning and thinking skills (PLTS)

The skills and qualities that improve your ability to work independently and be more effective and confident at work. Opportunities for developing these are a feature of all BTEC First courses. They aren't compulsory to achieve on the course, but are of great use to you.

Plagiarism

Copying someone else's work or work from any other sources (eg the internet) and passing it off as your own. It is strictly forbidden on all courses.

Portfolio

A collection of work compiled by a learner – for an **assessor** – usually as evidence of learning.

Project

A comprehensive piece of work which normally involves original research and planning and investigation, either by an individual or a team. The outcome will vary depending upon the type of project undertaken. For example, it may result in the organisation of a specific event, a demonstration of a skill, a presentation, or a piece of writing.

Tutorial

An individual or small group meeting with your tutor at which you discuss the work you are currently doing and other more general course issues.

Unit content

Details about the topics covered by the unit and the knowledge and skills you need to complete it.

Work placement

Time spent on an employer's premises when you carry out work-based tasks as an employee and also learn about the enterprise to develop your skills and knowledge.

Work-related qualification

A qualification designed to help you to develop the knowledge and understanding you need for a particular area of work.